MILLER'S

sci-fi &
Fantasy Collectibles

MILLER'S

sci-fi &
Fantasy Collectibles

Phil Ellis

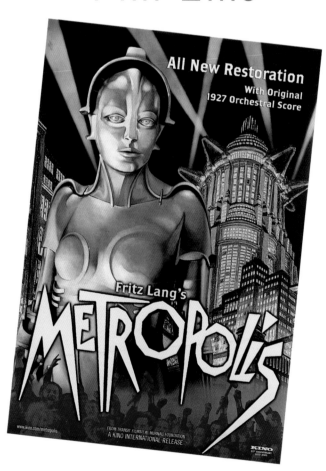

Miller's Sci-Fi & Fantasy Collectibles
Phil Ellis

First published in Great Britain in 2003 by Miller's,
an imprint of Octopus Publishing Group Ltd, 2–4 Heron Quays, London E14 4JP

Miller's is a registered trademark of Octopus Publishing Group Ltd

© 2003 Octopus Publishing Group Ltd

Commissioning Editor	Anna Sanderson
Executive Art Editor	Rhonda Fisher
Senior Editor	Emily Anderson
Design	Vicky Short, Victoria Bevan
Editor	Catherine Blake
Proofreader	Claire Musters
Indexer	Sue Farr
Production	Sarah Rogers
Special Photography	Steve Tanner, Robin Saker

ISBN 1 84000 729 X

A CIP record for this book is available from the British Library

Set in Granjon and Helvetica
Produced by Toppan Printing Co., (HK) Ltd.
Printed and bound in China

To order this book as a gift or an incentive contact Mitchell Beazley on 020 7531 8481

Front jacket, clockwise from top left: Captain Kirk action figure by Mego, 1970s, (£50–100/$75–150); 1960s tinplate Planet Explorer by Nomura, Japan (£120–160/$180–240); *Thunderbirds are Go* LP (£70–100/$105–150); *Dr Who* battery-operated Dalek by Marx, 1960s (£70–80/$105–120); *Star Wars* soap by Cliro, 1970s (£5–10/$7.50–15); **Back jacket:** Darth Vader large boxed action figure, 30cm/12in high (£110–160/$165–240)
Half-Title page: Atomic Rocket toy by Masudaya, 1950s (£400–500/$600–750)
Title page: Double-sided UK poster for the 2002 re-release of *Metropolis* (£30–50/$45–75)
This page: Billiken National Kid tinplate wind-up robot, 1990s (£80–100/$120–150)

Contents

Introduction

It is no accident that interest in science-fiction and fantasy has grown alongside technology. Many scientists admit to having gained inspiration from sci-fi, while technology in turn inspires fiction. Fantasy in all its forms, meanwhile, offers a respite from an increasingly complex world.

As for the history of these genres, it is difficult to know where to begin. Some consider Mary Shelley's *Frankenstein* to be the first true science-fiction novel, while others argue that fantasy has its roots in ancient mythology. Nineteenth-century novelists such as Jules Verne and H.G. Wells have certainly played their part, but the collection of toys, books, objects, and artifacts related to sci-fi and fantasy is a phenomenon very much of our own time.

The main impetus behind this collecting, suitably enough for a genre that depends on magic or technology for its appeal, is the magic and technology of television and cinema. While this book does include sci-fi and fantasy collectibles that have no obvious big- or small-screen connection, these are generally the exceptions. There are two reasons for this: firstly, TV and movie characters, and stories, reach a wider audience, and, secondly, movie studios and TV companies have an interest in promoting them. The shows and movies generate demand for merchandise, and the merchandise promotes the movies and shows.

The market for science-fiction and fantasy collectibles seems to be ever-expanding, because new shows are being made all the time. *Buffy the Vampire Slayer* became a huge international hit in the late 1990s and is still extremely popular. Yet its related merchandise has simply joined a whole host of collectibles from countless series of the past, and if you walk round a collectors' fair today you will find that *Buffy* items are now surrounded by collectibles from more recent shows.

Even when a show is cancelled, it lives on through video releases and repeats, and in the age of satellite and cable it is easy for a show to achieve immortality. Even the oldest ones attract new generations of followers, and merchandise is produced to cater for these fans; but for those who are old enough to remember them, the originals will probably always be the best.

Nevertheless, the younger fans who may have been introduced to *Thunderbirds* through the repeats of the early 1990s rather than the original late '60s screenings have an important role to play in the sci-fi and fantasy collectibles market. Of course, a large part of this market is driven by 30- and 40-somethings wanting to buy a piece of their childhood. Most people flipping through this book will at some point cry "I had one of those!", following this very often with a sigh of dismay as the realization of its current value dawns. But the younger collectors will maintain interest in the shows and the collectibles that go with them for the foreseeable future – and will in turn introduce their own offspring to this fascinating corner of the collectible world.

Star Wars and *Star Trek* are very well represented in this book and I make no apologies for this. *Star Wars* and *Star Trek* (not necessarily in that order), probably followed by *Doctor*

○ **£**4.000-5.000
○ **$**6.000-7.500

⬆ This plastic PEZ space gun dates from the late '50s/early '60s and, while it has a gold finish, it is literally worth many times its weight in gold. The space gun shape was manufactured in several different colours, but gold was reserved for a special mail offer. It was first available in Europe in the 1940s and in the US from 1953 and is the most desirable of all PEZ dispensers. This example sold for £4,160/$6,250 on Ebay in 2002.

Who and the shows of Gerry Anderson, have the largest following among sci-fi and fantasy fans. However, *Star Wars* and *Star Trek* are definitely the "big two", with far more followers than all the rest. Consequently, there are collectibles in abundance for these two, and recent claims that interest is on the wane should be taken with a large pinch of salt.

Finally, there are a few points about the guide prices quoted in this book. For a grouped picture the prices are for each separate item, unless stated otherwise. Many are recent auction results, while others are average values from different sales. All are rough guides only, because values can be extremely volatile; a new movie based on a series or character can boost interest, and thus the value, of any relevant collectibles. Note also that prices can also vary according to condition – it has been assumed that items are in excellent condition unless stated otherwise. However, remember that the value of any object depends entirely on what a person will pay for it.

Timeline

1900–1929

○ 1902 – Georges Méliès releases *A Trip to the Moon*, regarded as the first ever sci-fi film

○ 1905 – Einstein publishes his Special Theory of Relativity

○ 1921 – Czech author Karel Capek's play *Rossum's Universal Robots* features the concept of machines made to resemble human beings

○ 1921 – Gene Roddenberry, creator of *Star Trek*, is born

○ 1926 – *Metropolis*, Fritz Lang's ground-breaking movie, is released

○ 1929 – *Thunderbirds* creator Gerry Anderson is born

1930–1939

○ 1930 – Discovery of the planet Pluto

○ 1933 – The movie *King Kong* is released

○ 1937 – First edition of J.R.R. Tolkien's *The Hobbit* is published

○ 1938 – Controversial broadcast of H.G. Wells' *War of the Worlds* on American radio is mistaken for a news report by many listeners, who fear a Martian invasion

○ 1938 – Superman makes his debut in *Action Comics*

○ 1939 – Batman first appears in *DC Comics*

1940–1959

○ 1945 – Nuclear weapons are used for the first time

○ 1949 – George Orwell's book *1984* is published

○ 1950 – Dan Dare makes his first comic-book appearance

○ 1954 – *The Lord of the Rings* is first published

○ 1957 – Space Age dawns as Russians launch *Sputnik*, the first artificial satellite

⬆ A scene from the 1902 Georges Méliès movie, *A Trip to the Moon*, its subject – lunar exploration – seemed fantastic at the time.

⬆ The launch of the first artificial satellite in 1957 prompted many toys, including this Sputnik launching pad by Rodados Brillo of Argentina.

1960–1969   1970–1979   1980–1989   1990–2003

○ 1961 – Yuri Gagarin becomes the first man in space

○ 1962 – Spiderman makes his first appearance in the *Amazing Fantasy* comic

○ 1963 – *Doctor Who* debuts on British television, the day after the assassination of John F. Kennedy

○ 1964 – *Stingray* is broadcast – the first British show to be made in colour, even though colour TV was not available in the UK at the time

○ 1965 – *Thunderbirds* debuts on UK television

○ 1966 – *Star Trek* debuts on American television

○ 1967 – World's first heart transplant is performed in South Africa

○ 1968 – The movie *2001: A Space Odyssey* is released

○ 1968 – First version of *Planet of the Apes* film is released

○ 1969 – Neil Armstrong becomes the first man on the moon; *Star Trek* debuts on British television in the same week

○ 1976 – Viking probe sends back pictures from the surface of Mars

○ 1976 – Concorde brings first supersonic passenger jet service

○ 1977 – George Lucas' film *Star Wars* is released

○ 1978 – First test-tube baby is born; *Hitch-Hiker's Guide to the Galaxy* is broadcast on BBC radio

○ 1979 – *Star Trek* hits the big screen for the first time

○ 1980s – Micro-chips bring about a personal computer revolution

○ 1981 – Space Shuttle's first mission

○ 1982 – The film *Blade Runner* is released

○ 1986 – *Challenger* Space Shuttle disaster

○ 1997 – Dolly the cloned sheep is born

○ 1997 – *Buffy the Vampire Slayer* makes its TV debut

○ 1999 – *Star Wars* series revived with *The Phantom Menace*

○ 2000 – Decoding of the human genome

○ 2003 – *Columbia* Space Shuttle disaster

⬆ Sixteen years after the original *Star Wars* trilogy ended, the series returned in 1999 with *The Phantom Menace*, to continue the saga for a whole new generation.

⬆ The reality of lunar exploration in 1969, as an astronaut descends from his Apollo lunar module to begin exploring the moon's surface.

Action Figures

Some people say that action figures were first made in an attempt by the toy companies to sell dolls to boys, but this is only partly true. It would perhaps be more accurate to describe them as a half-way house between dolls and the toy soldiers that have been resident in toy boxes the world over for generations. Today's market is a very sophisticated one and new figures are being released all the time, driven by new films and television shows. Traditionally it is the heroes that have been produced in the greatest numbers, mainly because they are preferred by the young audience at which these figures are targeted. As a result they are generally not so scarce nor, therefore, as valuable as the villains. Female figures are a good choice if you are looking for promising collectibles, as usually they are produced in fewer numbers. Minor characters are also a good investment as again fewer are made, and some become cult figures among fans.

Star Wars

Star Wars has been credited with changing so many things, and some of the claims made for it are perhaps a little exaggerated. However, it is no exaggeration to say that it changed the action-figure market forever. Star Wars introduced action figures that were smaller than the market had been used to (so that they could fit into toy spacecraft), and they came with moulded-on clothing. Collectors prefer the figures to be "carded" – on the original card that formed the packaging. The first 12 figures produced had the 12 characters on the back of the card. For this reason, these early figures are often called "12 backs", and they are usually the most valuable. The addition of further characters to the range created "20 backs", and so on. Prices can be quite volatile, but these figures have usually proved to be sound investments and there is every reason to suppose that this will continue as further movies are released. As well as the older figures, rarities are also valuable. European editions may be hard to find in the USA but not in Europe, and vice versa. Sometimes, later production runs included variations or errors, which make them worth more, but beware of fakes such as the Jawa figures. A few of the Jawa figures were given vinyl instead of cloth capes, making them rare and sought-after – but it is not difficult to add a vinyl cape to a loose figure.

◖ Darth Vader is perhaps the best-known villain in sci-fi, and makes an exception to the rule that says young fans are less interested in the villains. Even though this 8cm/3in example is one of the original issues, it is only worth about £10/$15 as a loose figure; packaging is not only desirable in itself, but it also contains useful information that helps to date the figure. With its packaging, an early issue can fetch as much as £150–200/$225–300.

○ **£**8–12
○ **$**12–18

○ **£**5–10
○ **$**7.50–15

➤ Greedo is only a minor figure in Star Wars, meeting his end early in the film at the hands of Han Solo. Nonetheless he still merits an action figure, not least because something of a cult has grown up around this hapless bounty hunter. This early figure is quite desirable, but his gun is missing and, like the Darth Vader figure, he is not "carded"; with gun and on his card he would easily be worth ten times as much as the sum quoted.

"a long time ago, in a galaxy far, far away..."

➡ Boba Fett was a bounty hunter, but a more successful one than Greedo. He was the 21st figure to be made, and consequently his addition created the "21 back" packaging. The 21-back Boba Fett is highly sought-after, and, with packaging, prices can run into the hundreds. Variations and errors are known on Boba Fett figures, so collectors tend to pay particularly close attention to them. An especially desirable Boba Fett is a rocket-firing 30cm/12in pre-production model, which failed safety tests and so was never put into production. However, some are on the market and have sold at auction for as much as £400/$600.

○ **£140–160**
○ **$210–240**

◀ Chewbacca is one of the most popular *Star Wars* figures, so many versions were produced, although this particular version was not made in such quantities as many others. This is a large (40cm/16in) action figure, and was in some ways a victim of Kenner's own success in introducing smaller-sized figures. After all, you could buy several smaller Chewies for the price of a large version, and children (and parents) understood this. While some consider the quality of the moulding to be disappointing, this figure did have nice movable joints and a crossbow.

○ **£350–550**
○ **$525–825**

➡ These figures, produced in 1980–2, were made for *The Empire Strikes Back*. Although they are loose, they have their accessories and, most importantly, are in good condition. (If the packaging is badly damaged, a figure may not fetch much more than if it were loose.) In the mid-1980s, a line of figures under the name "The Power of the Force" was released, the last for ten years. Some of the most sought-after *Star Wars* figures are those from the "Early Bird" package – a special mail offer issued before the movie's release.

○ **£5–10**
○ **$7.50–15**

Cult TV

Although *Star Wars* revolutionized the market in action figures, a thriving market for figures spawned by popular television shows already existed. However, unlike *Star Wars* figures, which were available from the outset, models related to classic cult TV shows, such as *Star Trek* and *Doctor Who*, sometimes took a while to appear in the shops. While characters from cult TV shows are not always well-known to the general public, there are exceptions – everyone has heard of the time-travelling doctor, or Mr Spock. Nevertheless, this hasn't stopped action-figure manufacturers from taking serious liberties: some early figures of Tom Baker's Doctor Who used the head of Gareth Hunt from a *New Avengers* line! As with all action figures, those in their original packaging will always be more desirable than loose examples. Bear in mind, too, that the stars of the show are not necessarily stars in the collecting world, because they are likely to have been made in greater numbers. Kirk is certainly "beamed up" by collectors, but not with the same enthusiasm as some of the rarer figures. Incidentally, *Star Trek* fans (whether they be called Trekkies or Trekkers) will tell you that he never actually said "Beam me up Scottie", although the phrase has now become part of the English language.

○ **£**125–150
○ **$**190–225

"Beam me up Scottie"

○ **£**30–40
○ **$**45–60

↑ Mego is one of the great names in action figures, but the company sadly went out of business some years ago. Its *Star Trek* figures appeared in 1974, when the now largely forgotten Filmation animated series was being shown. These figures were first produced with just five characters on the packaging – the ones top right are from the second issue, when Uhura was added. All are collectible, but the first issues are more desirable. Dr McCoy and Scottie usually sell for more than Spock, Kirk, or the Klingon (left), but the rarer aliens command premium prices. An Andorian or Romulan from the third series, issued in 1976, can sell for £500/$750.

⬆ The ERTL company was founded in the United States by a German immigrant in 1945, and soon developed a reputation for quality die-cast toys. The firm decided to enter the action-figure market in 1984 with a series of four figures based on *Star Trek III*. This figure of Captain Kirk is one of them; the others were for Spock, Scottie, and a Klingon with his pet Targ. The figures suffered from distribution problems, and they are difficult to find to this day.

⬆ As *Star Trek* was revived as "The Next Generation" television series, with spin-offs such as "Voyager" and "Deep Space Nine" to follow, so new figures appeared to cater for the demand from fans. By this time, the collectors' market was well-established, but manufacturers, such as Playmates, aimed to stimulate it further by producing limited-edition figures, such as this one of Reginald Barclay. Barclay was a fairly minor character but popular with fans, and this figure was limited to just 3,000 – making it worth ten times as much as a more common figure.

⬆ Doctor Who was played by several different actors, and Tom Baker (seen here) was among the most loved. The series was a huge international hit, and dolls were marketed with appropriate packaging to suit the country where the programme was being shown. This figure, from Harbert toy company, dates from the 1970s and was for the Italian market.

⬆ Doctor Who had many assistants in the 25+ years that the programme was in production, and while Mel was not one of the most popular with the fans, she still merited an action figure. This one, dating from 1987, was made by Dapol, who won the rights to produce Dr Who figures in the late 1980s. There were two versions of Mel – this one, and another with a pink blouse; the pink version is slightly more valuable.

1970s–'80s

○ £ 115–135
○ $ 175–205

The manufacture of *Star Wars* figures in a smaller size was not the only innovation during the 1970s and '80s – these decades also saw the burgeoning of the action-figure market. Inventive manufacturers included Mego, a company that introduced the idea of interchangeable bodies. This cut production costs and reduced losses in the case of failed toy lines (which, however, didn't save the firm from eventual bankruptcy). It was during these years, of course, that sci-fi and fantasy achieved mainstream success with movies and TV shows that would continue to inspire action figures into the 1990s and beyond. It was a time that saw the appearance of some memorable characters, from revivals such as *Buck Rogers* to newcomers such as *Alien*. One thing that you should always bear in mind is that the action-figure market can be volatile, and prices can rise and fall. Sometimes this is because a large number of figures has just come on to the market, but sometimes fluctuations can reflect the changing popularity, or otherwise, of particular characters and toy lines. It is also worth remembering that some figures may be worth more in the USA than in Europe, or vice versa, depending on how easy they are to find in that part of the world.

○ £ 75–85
○ $ 115–130

⬆ *Buck Rogers* started out as a 1930s comic strip, but the late '70s saw a movie and TV revival. Action figures followed, but only in two ranges: a small size, and the 30cm/12in figures shown here. They were quite well made, but the faces had a tendency to fade. Boxed and in good condition they are very desirable – especially the villainous Tigerman.

◀ *Battlestar Galactica* was one of the many contenders for a rival to *Star Wars*. The movie was fairly successful, as was the TV series, and Mattel produced a full line of figures with a nice selection of aliens to go with them, including villains such as this Ovion character. Unfortunately they were a little short on accessories, although this meant there was less to lose. The main problem with the Ovion figure is that its costume is rather flimsy and easily torn.

○ £ 10–15
○ $ 15–22

The Black Hole was an expensive flop, and Mego's accompanying toys, issued in two series, suffered accordingly. The first, more common, series featured Holland, Durant, Reinhart, Booth, McCrae, Maximillian, Pizer, and V.I.N.Cent, and the second, Humanoid, Old B.O.B., S.T.A.R., and Sentry. The Sentry figure was the only one of the second wave to be released in the USA, so examples of the others are particularly desirable to American collectors – for example, a mint-condition Humanoid can fetch as much as $900.

○ £18-20
○ $27-30

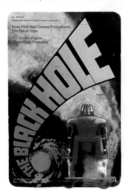

○ £15-25
○ $22-38

○ £150-200
○ $225-300

Alien (1979) was a huge box-office hit, but action-figure lines were relatively slow to emerge. Kenner did plan a line of 9cm/3½in figures for the first movie, but they were never issued – although a 45cm/18in Alien figure (much sought-after today) was briefly released. The first proper figures appeared in the 1980s; they were based on the second movie, which came out in 1986, and on the *Aliens* comic books, produced by Dark Horse. Kenner made more *Aliens* figures between 1992 and 1998, including the 30cm/12in Aliens/Corporal Hicks figure shown here. They were produced in a limited edition of 25,000. The 18cm/7in Ripley figure and newborn alien were made by Hasbro for *Alien Resurrection*, the fourth movie, in 1997.

○ £50-85
○ $75-130

He-Man and the Masters of the Universe was born when the United States repealed a law that banned programmes from being based on children's toys. Mattel and Filmation Associates responded with this hugely popular show. A movie and a new series have since maintained public interest. The extensive range of accompanying figures measured 13cm/5½in and set new standards with the introduction of "action features" (with transforming, moving parts). He-Man himself was made in large numbers and so is not as valuable as other characters.

1990s

The growth of the collecting market meant that by the 1990s just about every new movie or TV series with a sci-fi or fantasy theme had to have a range of figures to accompany it. This obviously provided a great many opportunities for manufacturers as well. The decade also saw the dawning of an age of enlightenment in which it was no longer considered strange for grown-ups to want action-figure toys. While toys made for the kids were, and still are, collected by adults, new lines emerged that were made specifically for the adult market. Limited-edition figures are obvious examples of products made with adults in mind, not to mention future investment potential. Some fans find this cynical because it puts the figures out of reach of ordinary collectors – but maybe that's the point. The popularity of a series or film on which figures are based can be a two-edged sword. A series with a large following will have many fans vying for your collectibles, should you choose to sell. On the other hand, figures from a less successful show will have been produced in smaller numbers, giving them rarity value. In the end, the best advice can only be to buy the figures if you like the show.

"To infinit

○ **£** 60–80
○ **$** 90–120

⬆ *Toy Story* (1995) was the first fully computer-animated movie, but it will also be remembered for its major marketing blunder. Quite simply, demand for related toys, especially for the figure of Buzz Lightyear, seen here, was seriously underestimated; it became the toy of the year and every child wanted one. The very first versions, released in the autumn of 1995, featured a yellow stripe across the front of the box. This one is worth about 20 per cent more than those issued just a few months later. The guide price quoted here is for the earlier version, in its original box.

○ **£** 8–12
○ **$** 12–18

⬅ In 1997, the "Men in Black" came to save Earth from "the Scum of the Universe". Pictured here is Agent Jay; while there can be little doubt that fans of the movie enjoyed the figures, many serious collectors felt that the quality and detail weren't particularly impressive. The figures made for the sequel were generally better received. Sadly, the sequel itself wasn't as good as the original movie, but then you can't have everything.

and beyond!"

- ◯ **£**350-400
- ◯ **$**525-600

➡ Tim Burton's *Nightmare Before Christmas* was one of the surprise cinema hits of 1993, thanks to its imaginative storyline and the persona of its hero (or antihero), the weird but well-meaning Jack Skellington. It certainly captured the imagination of the public, and a range of figures appeared for various characters in the movie. Because it was a hit with adults as well as children – indeed, possibly even more so – many figures were made with adult collectors in mind. This large 1.2m/47in figure was made in 1998 in a limited edition of just 800, hence its high value.

⬅ During the 1990s, Playmates won the licence to produce figures for *Star Trek: The Next Generation* and also for spin-offs such as *Voyager* and *Deep Space Nine*. Seen here is a figure of Benjamin Sisko, commander of the DS9 space station. Sisko is one of the more common figures, but Playmates produced some in limited editions. One example is the character of Lt Reginald Barclay from the *Voyager* series, which was limited to an edition of just 3,000, and can fetch £150/$225 or more (*see page 15*).

- ◯ **£**10-20
- ◯ **$**15-30

- ◯ **£**25-30
- ◯ **$**38-45

➡ When Mego made the original *Planet of the Apes* figures in the 1970s, it did not appear to have included a figure based on Taylor, the Charlton Heston character (perhaps because of contractural problems). Instead, alongside the apes, they produced a generic "astronaut" figure. Later, there was a series based closely on the characters from the TV show. The 30cm/12in high figures shown here are from a special "collector's edition" series issued by Hasbro in 1999, and this time Taylor is featured, shown here with a gorilla soldier.

Books & Annuals

Since the days of Jules Verne and H.G. Wells, science-fiction and fantasy have kept the publishers busy and the presses rolling. However, many argue that it was not these writers but the comic books of the 1930s that really created the market for fantasy and sci-fi books as we know it. Books generally need to be first editions to achieve any real value, but there are exceptions: even a mundane copy in its umpteenth edition can be worth a substantial amount if it bears an inscription by the author. This is especially true if the inscription is very personal, or offers an insight into the writer, rather than simply a signature. Collectors have been known to focus on a specific title, acquiring every edition – including foreign language issues; this is just one of many "niche" markets. Annuals, meanwhile, were once frowned on by mainstream book collectors (and still are, to an extent) but as the sci-fi and fantasy market develops, and certain annuals begin to fetch high prices, attitudes are changing.

Publishers

Fantasy and science-fiction have always had to endure a degree of intellectual snobbery; indeed, science-fiction writers had great difficulty getting published at all in the first half of the 20th century. In the early years, nobody even called it "science-fiction" – the term was coined in the 1920s by Hugo Gernsbach, editor of *Amazing Stories* (the Hugo Award for the best sci-fi writing is named after him). Because mainstream publishers would not consider science-fiction novels for publication, fresh opportunities for enterprising new publishers opened up to fill the gap. The public demand for sci-fi certainly existed, as subsequent history has shown. Today, many mainstream publishers include sci-fi on their lists, but because of their important place in the history and development of the genre, books from the early specialist publishers are prized by collectors. Names to look out for in this field include Fantasy Press, Gnome Press, and Ballantine; titles by these and many other publishers are sought-after as much because of the publisher as the author. After all, if it hadn't been for some of these publishers, the great names in sci-fi might never have been given their big break.

Written in 1950, *The Dying Earth* by Jack Vance (the pen name of John Holbrook Vance) is a tale of life in the distant future, when magic and science are interchangeable. Lancer is a much admired imprint; it specialized in re-issues of sci-fi and fantasy classics, as well as developing a good selection of its own original titles, many of which were quite inventive. This publisher also introduced limited editions of various titles in an attempt to attract a more discerning buyer, although this was not particularly successful.

○ **£** 5–8
○ **$** 7.50–12

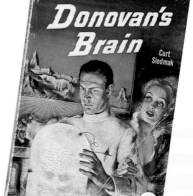

○ **£** 4–8
○ **$** 6–12

Corgi is known as a non-specialist publisher, but it nevertheless produced some excellent editions that have become quite collectible – even the ubiquitous Penguin has its followers in this area of paperback collecting. Bantam first published *Donvan's Brain*, the story of a man whose brain is taken over by another, in 1950. The 1952 Corgi UK version, shown here, has identical cover artwork.

Most collectors have a soft spot for the Ace Doubles, and early examples of this particular title are avidly collected. Ace offered two complete novels, bound back-to-back, so when you have finished reading one, you can simply turn the book over and start on the second. This title was bound with *Conan the Conqueror*. Many great writers, including Isaac Asimov, Philip K. Dick, and Poul Anderson, were published in early Ace Doubles. One way to tell that this is an early edition is the cover price: by the end of the 1950s, the price had increased to 50 cents.

○ **£** 4-5
○ **$** 6-7.50

○ **£** 10-20
○ **$** 15-30

Ballantine Books was founded by Ian Ballantine in 1953 with the aim of treating sci-fi as literature, rather than pulp fiction. Consequently, he planned to issue books in hardback as well as paperback, although few Ballantine books were actually published in hardback so those that were are especially valuable. This is an American Ballantine paperback from 1957 of John Wyndham's classic tale of terror, better known as the 1960 film, *Village of the Damned*, starring George Sanders. A first edition of this book can sell for as much as ten or twenty times the price quoted for this example.

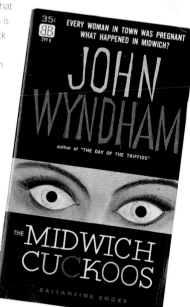

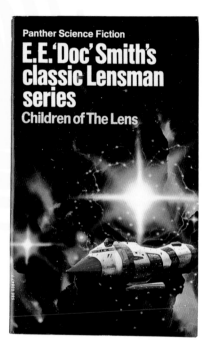

Children of The Lens is the sixth novel in the Lensman series by E.E. "Doc" Smith, one of the most popular science-fiction writers. The Fantasy Press editions published in the 1950s are well known, but this is a 1973 edition published by Panther, a British firm. Panther, along with Sphere and Arrow, established a fine international reputation for producing attractive and appealing editions characterized by great attention to detail, good print quality, and superb cover artwork. British publishers have become something of a niche market with American collectors, who appreciate their high production values.

○ **£** 4-6
○ **$** 6-9

Authors

Many of the points that can be made about collecting science-fiction books apply equally to books in general. First editions of a debut novel by an author who went on to become famous tend to be the most valuable. The latest blockbuster by an author who already has several successful novels under his or her belt is unlikely to be as valuable because there will be many more copies available. For some reason, book-club editions never seem to sell for very much, even if they are first editions. Signed first editions are especially desirable, particularly if the author's inscription is more than just a signature. An interesting development of recent years is that many sci-fi authors have now achieved a degree of respectability in mainstream literary circles. However, one suspects that Asimov, Vonnegut, and Philip K. Dick will never achieve quite the same mainstream kudos as E.M. Forster, D.H. Lawrence, or Thomas Hardy, which seems a pity. There are many collectible sci-fi authors, and only a handful can be represented here.

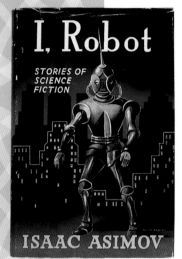

The Russian-born American writer Isaac Asimov is often regarded as one of the greatest ever science-fiction writers. *I, Robot* is one of his best works, introducing, as it does, his "laws of robotics" that govern the relationships between robots and humans. It is not, strictly speaking, a novel – rather a collection of connected short stories and novellas that became hugely influential. Asimov was one of the greats to be published by Gnome Press; a first edition from 1950 is very valuable if it is in fine condition, complete with its dust jacket.

○ £500–1,000
○ $750–1,500

○ £70–80
○ $105–120

Philip K. Dick was one of many well-known authors whose works were published in the "Ace Doubles" series. These books featured two complete novels, bound back-to-back. This edition of *The Man Who Japed* was published in 1956 and was bound with E.C. Tubb's *The Space Born*. Dick's complex prose and outlandish tales have won him legions of fans (many of whom call themselves "Dick heads"). Any of his works are collectible, the early ones especially so. These Ace editions are sought-after in themselves, and the inclusion of a first printing of a Philip K. Dick story adds value.

○ **£** 8-12
○ **$** 12-18

➥ John Wyndham is probably best known for writing *The Day of the Triffids*, but he has achieved his place in the sci-fi hall of fame through a series of thoughtful, well-written novels; one such is *Trouble with Lichen*. Wyndham tends to be more interested in people than in detailed studies of future technology. This book raises the question of what would happen if our lifespan could be increased dramatically. The jacket of this 1960 Ballantine paperback is by the celebrated cover artist Richard M. Powers, providing illustrator as well as author interest.

○ **£** 4-6
○ **$** 6-9

⬇ His founding of the Church of Scientology has made L. Ron Hubbard a controversial figure, but this should not detract from his undoubted status as one of the most widely read and collected sci-fi authors. He is also one of the most influential. *Final Blackout* was written in 1940 and imagined a future in which World War II continued until 1975. This paperback edition, with cover art by Nick Galloway, was published in 1970.

○ **£** 8-12
○ **$** 12-18

↟ *The Sirens of Titan*, published in 1959, has been hailed as a masterpiece, and prompted one critic to note that Vonnegut used the novel not only to ask the question of the meaning of life but also to answer it. It is the novel that truly established his reputation; his satirical chaotic universe full of tragic-comic events has won him legions of admirers. This coronet edition dates from 1967 and isn't particularly valuable, but hardback first editions have been known to reach four-figure sums.

1950s Paperbacks

The science-fiction market was still in its infancy before World War II, and during the war paper was in short supply and reserved for essentials. This helps to explain why the post-war period came to be regarded as a "golden age" for sci-fi publishing. The ten or so years in book publishing from the early 1950s to the early '60s reflect the almost contemporary "Silver Age" that comics collectors enthuse about. Even so, science-fiction and fantasy publishing as we understand it didn't really get underway in paperback until 1953, when publishers such as Ace and Ballantine entered the fray. The paperback revolution undoubtedly helped to fuel an already existing public appetite for futuristic fiction in an age when atomic energy and rockets promised so much. Paperbacks were cheap, and, because of the snobbery against the genre, works by many now-famous writers were published first in this format. Sadly, many of the pioneering speciality publishers of sci-fi paperbacks in the 1950s eventually became victims of their own success, as mainstream publishers with better financial resources at their disposal moved into the market.

The Blonde Goddess of Bal-Sagoth was written by Robert E. Howard, author of the Conan books, which are perhaps known to most through the Arnold Schwarzenegger movies. This book was published in 1950 in the highly collectible Avon Fantasy series; classic 1950s books, the Avon titles had some first-rate authors and some superb covers. Paperbacks are naturally less well protected than hardbacks, and condition is always important; in fine condition, this book can sell for £30/$45 or more.

○ **£**25-35
○ **$**38-52

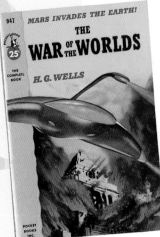

○ **£**10-15
○ **$**15-22

The 1950s was a time when "alien invasion" stories found a receptive audience – largely, perhaps, because of Cold War paranoia. However, H.G. Wells' invaders were not from the Red Army, but from the Red Planet, and his tale, dating from 1898, is one of the most famous sci-fi stories of all time. This edition was published in 1953 by Pocket Books to coincide with the release of George Pal's movie, which updated the action to the present day. A first edition might set you back £1,000/$1,500, but a classic 1950s paperback edition is still very desirable, and much more affordable.

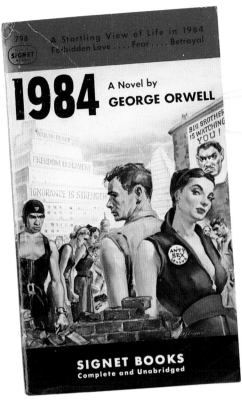

This nightmare vision of the future, written by George Orwell, aka Eric Blair, was published in 1949. He did not, of course, live to experience the real nightmares of 1984 (the fashions that year!) because he died in 1950, the year in which this paperback edition appeared. Published by Signet, and with cover art by Alan Harmon, it is of interest because it is the first paperback edition of this now famous novel. Orwell has a great literary reputation, so collecting interest extends beyond the fans of 1950s paperbacks.

○ **£** 90-100
○ **$** 135-150

○ **£** 25-35
○ **$** 38-52

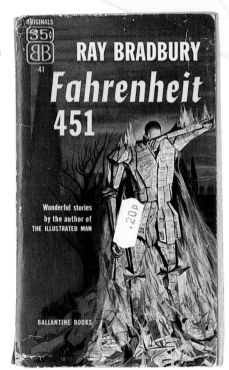

Robert Heinlein's *The Man Who Sold the Moon* is the first in his fabled "future history" series. Heinlein is a collected author, but in addition this Pan paperback from 1955 is a good example of the growing interest of mainstream publishers in science-fiction. Heinlein's works were also published by specialist science-fiction publishers such as Fantasy Press and Gnome. Paperback editions were issued by various publishers throughout the 1950s, so if you wish to base your collection on the paperback editions of one writer from this decade, Heinlein is a good candidate.

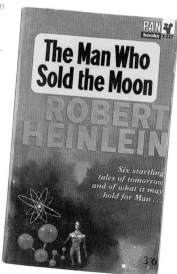

○ **£** 8-12
○ **$** 12-18

Ray Bradbury's *Fahrenheit 451* first appeared in a 1950 magazine under the title of "The Fireman". This Ballantine paperback dates from 1953 and was the true first edition of this book, which is regarded as one of the landmarks in science-fiction; the hardback edition was published by Ballantine a month and a half later. This copy is not in the best condition: there is a fair amount of wear, and it bears a price sticker from a secondhand bookshop. However, it is a very collectible edition of an important work, so in fine condition could fetch as much as £100/$150.

Illustrators

They say that you should never judge a book by its cover – but of course, "they" are sometimes wrong, and never more so than in the field of science-fiction and fantasy. Thanks to its magazine, comic, and "pulp fiction" heritage, the genre can boast some superb examples of artists' skill, and many books have their collectible appeal considerably enhanced by a really good cover. Sometimes, books are collected primarily for the cover art, and many collectors have their favourite illustrators. If this sounds strange to the uninitiated, then it should be remembered that the market has a great many, far more esoteric, niches – some book collectors even specialize in editions that include maps of fictional places referred to in the text. Illustrators to look out for include Richard Powers, Frank Frazetta, Jack Kirby, and Ric Binkley, but there are many, many more. As with movie posters, the purpose of cover art is to grab one's attention, and the most popular illustrators produced some eye-popping artwork. Sometimes the covers seem to be only vaguely connected to events in the story, but that's half the fun.

This 1955 Gnome Press edition of the *Tales of Conan* was finished by the writer and editor Sprague de Camp after Conan the Barbarian's creator Robert E. Howard had died. Illustrator Wallace Wood worked for many comic book publishers, including DC, Marvel, and Warren, and edited his own "underground" publication, *Witzend*, but committed suicide in 1981, unable to cope with his continuing kidney disease. The copy shown here is signed by de Camp, but even an unsigned copy with its dust jacket is valuable.

○ £ 70-100
○ $ 105-150

○ £ 8-12
○ $ 12-18

Aldous Huxley's *Brave New World* is a compelling tale of life 600 years in the future. This 1952 edition, issued by the well-known publishers Bantam, features a cover illustration by Charles Binger, who produced jackets for many science-fiction and fantasy publications during the 1950s. Although readers may be forgiven for thinking that the cover is a somewhat loose interpretation of the story, to say the least, it is a superb illustration, and a fine example of Binger's work.

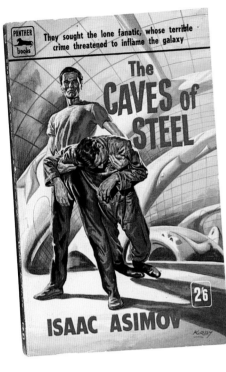

○ **£**8-12
○ **$**12-18

A classic sci-fi/murder mystery, the plot of Isaac Asimov's *The Caves of Steel* concerns the strange death of a robotics specialist. This Panther edition from 1958 boasts cover art by Jack Kirby, the great comic-strip artist, writer, and editor. Kirby, whose career spanned 50 years, is probably better known for his work for Marvel Comics. Interest in Kirby's work is huge, and editions such as this are as likely to be sought out by comic-book fans as by collectors interested in book illustration.

○ **£**4-6
○ **$**6-9

Frank Frazetta is one of the most prolific, best-known, and most influential of all fantasy artists, starting his career at the age of 16 and producing the artwork for numerous comics from the 1940s onwards. His talents were recognized in 1966 when he received the Hugo Award for best illustrator. This is a 1967 New English Library reprint of an Ace edition, and features a cover that typifies the life and drama that Frazetta put into his art.

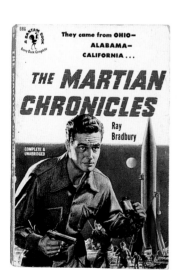

○ **£**18-22
○ **$**27-33

The Martian Chronicles is one of Ray Bradbury's most famous works, and a 1950 Doubleday edition with a green binding can be worth as much as £750/$1,125. This Bantam edition from 1951 is the first paperback edition and is much more affordable – it also has the bonus of a great cover. Unfortunately, the illustration is unsigned, but even if we cannot identify the artist, it is still an appealing book. Already collectible as the first-edition paperback, the book has a cover that is also attractive to connoisseurs of sci-fi and fantasy art.

Movie & TV Tie-ins

Fans of science-fiction and fantasy movies like to re-live their favourites in book form, so novelizations are always popular. Books based on movies and TV shows sell well, although they are usually bought by fans of the series rather than by serious collectors of the genre. They also tend to have quite large print runs, so they are not particularly hard to find, and therefore not usually very valuable. Having said that, this makes them accessible and affordable for anyone wishing to form a collection based on their favourite characters or shows. Some TV and movie tie-ins are simply adaptations of episodes, but others are completely new stories based on the characters. There are also "the making of" books that are prized as reference material, and "technical manuals" based on sci-fi shows. The latter cater for the fans' desire to know how starships, etc would work in reality. One *Star Trek* anecdote tells of a writer for the show being asked by a fan how the "inertial dampeners" on the *Enterprise* actually work. "Very well, thank you," came the straightforward reply!

◀ *Star Trek* novels were being produced from the show's earliest days, but this "fotonovel" dates from 1977. Production of the show had long since ceased, and the first movie was still two years in the future, but regular repeat showings helped to guarantee continuing interest. There were ten stories in this series, which was published by Bantam Books, and they were all based on actual episodes. Writers include Harlan Ellison and Jerome Bixby.

○ £10-15
○ $15-22

▼ Stephen Spielberg's *Close Encounters of the Third Kind* was one of the great "must-see" movies of the 1970s. This paperback is the novelization of the movie, published by Dell, who also issued a "fotonovel". *Close Encounters* is a fondly remembered movie that, unfortunately, tends to be overshadowed by the other great Spielberg alien epic, *E.T.* The popularity of the film at the time meant that the novel was printed in large quantities, so copies are not especially valuable.

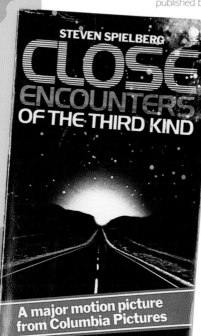

○ £4-6
○ $6-9

○ **£**4-6
○ **$**6-9

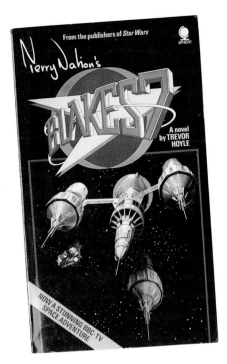

➡ *Blake's Seven* was created for the BBC by Terry Nation, who was also the man behind *Doctor Who*. The show was much ridiculed at the time for its wobbly sets and the variable performances, but it had (and still has) many followers. This is a first printing of the paperback by Trevor Hoyle, published by Sphere in 1977. Many more paperbacks followed, and they were still being printed years after the eponymous Blake and his crew were killed off on television in the early 1980s.

○ **£**5-7
○ **$**7.50-10.50

▌ *The Art of Tron*, written by Michael Bonifer, is considered a must for *Tron* fans. Published by Simon & Schuster, it is out of print now and not easy to find, especially outside the United States. It tells the story of its development, from the initial concept through to production, and offers an important insight into the making of this innovative movie. A valuable source of reference for the dedicated fan, it contains early sketches, logo designs, costume concepts, and much more. Reference books such as this are much sought-after if, as this one does, they contain information that's hard to find elsewhere.

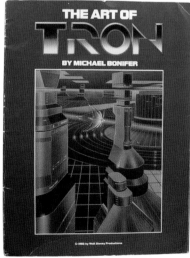

○ **£**35-45
○ **$**52-68

▲ "Do Androids Dream of Electric Sheep?" was the original title of the Philip K. Dick story on which the movie *Blade Runner* is based, so it's not hard to see why they decided on a title change. The movie tie-in paperback, published by Grafton, naturally used the movie title, but also referred to the original title on the cover, which featured the starring actor, Harrison Ford. This is a nice edition, and the cover artwork is great. What's more, it's much more affordable than a first-edition hardback, which pre-dates the movie by 14 years and can set you back £500-1,000/$750-1,500, or more.

Annuals

As the name suggests, annuals are books that appear every year, usually in the autumn to capture the Christmas market. They are generally forward-looking, so an annual for 1968 would have appeared in the run-up to Christmas 1967 and so on. Collectors look for as "clean" a copy as possible, and to be really desirable an annual should show no signs of damage (the spine is the most common casualty). It should be remembered that annuals were generally bought for children, who are not known for taking great care of books, so copies in good condition are often hard to find. Most annuals had the price printed in the corner of one of the inside pages – but if this has been clipped off it will affect the value. The annuals also usually included puzzles, games, and crosswords; ideally, these should be unmarked, but if they have been filled in, the annual can still be desirable depending on other factors, such as rarity value. Annuals are popular, not least because they include new stories that were not available in the comics on which they were based.

"Exterminate ... Exterminate"

○ **£**50–100
○ **$**75–150

It didn't take the BBC long to realize that in *Doctor Who* they had a major hit on their hands. The series made its debut late in 1963, and in 1964 *The Dalek Book* became the first Dalek annual. As such, it is much sought-after by *Doctor Who* fans, not least because of its superb colour artwork by Richard Jennings, who also drew the Daleks in the *TV21* comic. The next year saw a second annual, *The Dalek World*, which was followed the year after by *The Dalek Outer Space Book*. All three are desirable.

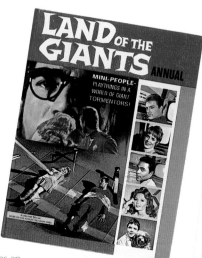

○ **£**10–20
○ **$**15–30

The TV series *Land of the Giants* was an Irwin Allen production dating from the late 1960s. As its title suggests, it was an intriguing yarn about a group of explorers who found themselves trapped on a world populated by giant-sized people, not to mention cats, dogs, and spiders! This annual was published in 1969 for 1970 by World Distributors and offers 94 colour pages of features and stories; a "TV storybook" was also issued in the same year.

The British comic *2000 AD*, published by Fleetway, was a truly groundbreaking publication and quickly attracted a large and loyal following, which it retains to this day. This 1979 annual was the second issued, and featured favourites such as Judge Dredd and Dan Dare. As an early annual in the series it is quite desirable, and it is difficult to find copies in very good condition. Annuals from different years can vary in price according to their availability. A 1989 annual in mint condition can sell for as much as £30/$45.

○ **£**5-10
○ **$**7.50-15

○ **£**20-25
○ **$**30-38

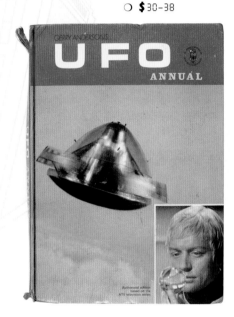

➡ Spiderman is one of the classic heroes who appeared in the early 1960s, in the so-called "Silver Age". The first *Spiderman* annual was published in 1964 and is much sought-after; a copy in very good condition can fetch £100–150/ $150–225. Pictured here is a 1983 annual, which is nowhere near as valuable, but fans of the Marvel comics superhero like to collect annuals from every year. If you have a copy to sell, your annual could well find a grateful buyer looking to fill a gap in his or her collection.

○ **£**5-10
○ **$**7.50-15

⬆ In the 1960s and '70s, the prevailing attitude was that puppet shows were for kids, so Gerry Anderson was delighted to have the chance to make *UFO*. It was not only his first live action series, but it was also given a peak slot on British television. Nevertheless, its hi-tech vehicles guaranteed the appreciation of a young audience and the annual reflects this. It was well-produced, and the wordiness of some of the stories suggests that it was not designed for the very young. These annuals do appear on the market, although they are not particularly common.

Comics & Graphic Novels

An avid comic collector once remarked that there was a reason why he had so many comics: from childhood, no-one had ever told him they were supposed to be thrown away. Many early comics are valuable precisely because so many *were* thrown away – only children ever thought of collecting them. Today things are different, and the rarest early comics can change hands for considerable sums. As paper collectibles they are particularly prone to wear and tear, especially if they have been in the grubby hands of several children. A copy in mint condition can be worth several times more than a copy in poor condition. A more recent phenomenon is the rise of the graphic novel, now a common sight in bookstores. From the outset of this genre, adult collectors have been active, and some authors and artists are avidly collected.

Golden & Silver Ages

This section is devoted to some of the superheroes who made their debuts during the "Golden" and "Silver" ages of comic production, although not all of the issues shown are necessarily from those periods. Although the terms are simple to understand, it is less easy to define the chronological boundaries because some enthusiasts have different views on when one era ends and another begins. Generally speaking, the "Golden Age" (sometimes abbreviated to "GA") runs from the late 1930s (many consider that it started with the publication of Action Comics in 1938), while the "Silver Age" runs from 1956 to 1969. The mid-1950s not only ushered in the Silver Age, but it also saw the founding of the Comics Code Authority (CCA), the industry's effort at self-policing, created to ensure that comics were suitable for their youth audience. Some collectors even refer to a "Platinum Age", to categorize comics that were published before 1938. Such very early comics are rare indeed, and they are not readily accessible to the vast majority of collectors. Most collectors start with the Silver Age, because comics from the Golden Age are becoming harder to find.

◀ DC (which stood for Detective Comics) was responsible for two of the world's greatest superheroes, Batman and Superman. The "bat man" concept is said to have been inspired by Leonardo da Vinci's drawings of flying machines, although in fact Batman lacked Superman's flying abilities. Batman made his comic-book debut in 1939, and the early issues are always desirable, especially if they feature popular villains. This is issue 84 from the first volume, one of the rarer issues. The cover features an early appearance by his charismatic adversary, Catwoman.

○ £275–325
○ $415–490

○ £4–6
○ $6–9

➡ As well as giving Batman to the world, DC was also responsible for Superman; the "Man of Steel" made his debut just before World War II, in 1938. His exploits were exciting enough in two dimensions, but here we have the chance to see him in 3-D, with the aid of a pair of special glasses – the 3-D craze was big in the cinemas in the early 1950s. The issue shown here is a more recent reprint, worth only a few pounds, but if you have an original 1953 issue it could be worth as much as £500/$750.

Spiderman, who first appeared in the early 1960s, was an unusual superhero. He was not from another planet and had no vast personal fortune; he was just a high-school student who obtained his powers by accident when he was bitten by an irradiated spider. "Spidey" frequently tackled controversial issues – in the '60s the Comics Code Authority withdrew its seal of approval because of a drugs-related storyline. This issue introduces the arch-villain Cyclone.

○ £40-60
○ $60-90

"Spiderman, Spiderman Does whatever a spider can"

Radioactivity, a recurring theme in the 1950s and '60s, also turned Bruce Banner into the Incredible Hulk. The comic first appeared in 1962 and lasted for six issues. Hulk then appeared in *Tales to Astonish*, until that comic was renamed *The Incredible Hulk* in 1968. For this reason, you will not find an *Incredible Hulk* comic from issue 7 to issue 101. This issue of *Tales to Astonish*, in which he shared the honours with Giant Man, was illustrated entirely by Steve Ditko, one of the greatest comic-book artists of all time, whose career spanned 45 years.

○ £50-70
○ $75-115

○ £40-60
○ $60-90

If Spiderman didn't have much going for him, then Daredevil arguably had even less. He was blinded in an accident involving nuclear waste, but found that his other senses were heightened considerably as a result. He went on to learn martial arts, which he used to good effect, along with his "radar sense". This issue, volume 12 issue 1, is of particular interest to collectors because it features the first work for Marvel by the popular artist John Romita. Collectors are frequently interested in such "firsts", which, in this case, makes the comic worth about £50/$75.

○ **£** 10–20
○ **$** 15–30

Iron Man made his Marvel Comics debut in 1963; he is the alter-ego of the industrialist Tony Stark, whose iron suit is both a life-support machine without which he would die, and a super-weapon. He was originally forced to develop the suit as a weapon for a Communist warlord in Vietnam, from whose clutches he escaped. On his return to the US, he used his suit and its powers to fight crime. This issue features the first appearance of Spymaster – a genius in industrial espionage, an expert assassin, and a saboteur extraordinaire.

KAPOW!

○ **£** 40–50
○ **$** 60–75

○ **£** 20–30
○ **$** 30–45

Some superheroes have powers that seem almost god-like; in the case of Marvel's Thor, that is because he is a god. The Norse god of thunder has been banished to Earth, where he takes on the persona of Jake Olsen – except, that is, when his considerable powers are needed. His main weapon is of course his hammer, which is also a means of flight. The character was originally one of the Avengers, along with other well-known Marvel favourites Iron Man and the Hulk. This is a bumper *Thor King-Size Special* dating from 1966, and its rarity value is reflected in the price.

The X-Men are a team of mutants with special powers, assembled by Professor Charles Xavier, himself a mutant, who helped them use and control their powers. Their aim is to combat evil mutants who mean to harm humanity. *X-Men* was created by Stan Lee and Jack Kirby in the early 1960s but, although it was unusual, it was not an immediate hit. Today, of course, *X-Men* is very popular due to recent feature films, so early titles are very collectible and can sell for considerable sums. This issue, which is of 1970s vintage, features the first *X-Men* artwork by British-born artist John Byrne, who went on to help revive the *Superman* series in the 1980s.

○ **£** 40-60
○ **$** 60-90

The Fantastic Four made their debut in the early 1960s; they gained their superpowers by accident after being irradiated during the test flight of a new spacecraft. Back on Earth, they decided to use their powers to combat any threats to Earth that were beyond the capabilities of conventional armed forces. This issue, from 1966, is desirable because it features the first appearance of the Black Panther, an African superhero. The inclusion of a black superhero at a time of unrest in the USA over civil rights adds historical interest.

○ **£** 110-130
○ **$** 165-195

DC Comics' *Justice League of America* is another example of how superheroes don't have to be loners and can team up to fight evil. Over the years, there have been various members of the League, as well as an earlier *Justice Society of America* dating back to the 1940s. This important title was made into a popular cartoon series, and the additional public exposure fuelled collector interest. This issue sees the first appearance of Doctor Destiny, evil genius and one of the League's most dangerous adversaries.

○ **£** 40-50
○ **$** 60-75

It was not unusual for heroes to appear first in other titles before getting their own dedicated comic. This was the case for Silver Surfer, who first appeared in *Fantastic Four* in 1966 before getting his own comic in 1968. Travelling on a "surfboard" endowed with special powers, he was originally a villain, sent to destroy Earth by the tyrant Galactus. However, he betrayed his master and finally took on the role of protector. The issue shown is one of a number that are hard to find, hence its value.

Bronze & Modern Ages

After the Golden and Silver ages come the Bronze and Modern; comic-collectors generally regard the "Bronze Age" as the 1970s, while the "Modern Age" begins around 1980 and continues to this day. Many Golden- and Silver-Age comics had relatively low print-runs (sometimes as few as 10,000), which means that they were comparatively rare to begin with. Most modern-day comics have far larger print-runs, of 100,000 and more, so in the future survivors should be far more common. Some disillusioned fans argue that commercial needs override artistic principles these days, and point to what they see as the "over-use" of popular characters by greedy publishers. Current issues of comic books are still collected, but never has the advice "buy what you like" been more pertinent. Collectible special limited-editions, variant covers, and printing errors will never generate the same excitement as tracking down a long lost title of the past, but it's impossible to write off the investment potential of modern comics completely. The industry has changed, but great art and good writing will always find admirers. It's also impossible to tell which of the characters currently being introduced will prove to be significant in the future.

○ £20–30
○ $30–45

🔺 Hailing from the planet Drakulon, and clearly owing much to the 1960s movie icon *Barbarella*, Vampirella first appeared in the summer of 1969, although the character truly blossomed in the '70s. Initially drawn by Frank Frazetta, she is a defender of mankind to this day, thanks to Harris Comics. She has a dedicated fanbase and interest has recently been rising. *Vampirella* straddles the sci-fi/fantasy/horror boundaries; this is issue 58, a Summer Special that is one of the rarest and most sought-after issues.

➡ The early 1970s saw a revival of interest in vampire stories, and a spate of "horror comics" with a supernatural theme. Although *Tomb of Dracula* was discontinued in 1979, Blade, the vampire hunter, lived on, not least in movies. He has one important advantage over his adversaries in that he is immune to the bite of the vampire, an immunity inherited from his mother, who was bitten by one of the creatures while giving birth. This issue is significant as it shows the origin of Blade.

○ £13–17
○ $20–25

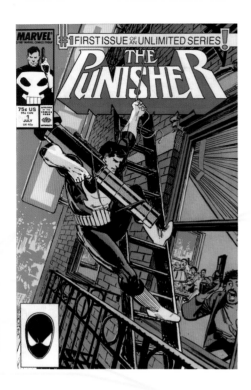

The Punisher made his first appearance as a Spiderman villain, but he became a hero in his own right and gained his own title. He is essentially a vigilante who turned to crime-fighting after the death of members of his family at the hands of criminals. This is the very first issue of *Punisher*, and it is quite scarce. His huge popularity in the late 1980s, which led to a film in 1990, began to wane afterwards; some fans attributed this to the over-exposure of guest appearances in other titles. A new movie is scheduled for 2004.

○ £ 8–12
○ $ 12–18

Excalibur is in some ways Britain's answer to the X-Men in that it is a team of crime-fighting mutants – and indeed some of the team *were* originally X-Men. Their leader is Captain Britain, who is ... well, Britain's answer to Captain America. Their base is a lighthouse off the British coast, and their unique tongue-in-cheek style makes them more than just a pale imitation of American heroes. This is the first issue, and while it is not worth a great deal at the moment, it is still worth rather more than its original 50p cover price.

○ £ 18–22
○ $ 27–33

 Wolverine is a mysterious mutant of indeterminate age and history, whose unique feature is the retractable claws emanating from his hands. Proof that Marvel superheroes are not always all-American (Wolverine is Canadian), he became a member of Charles Xavier's X-Men team. This issue is of historic importance to comic-book fans because it features our hero's first battle with Sabretooth, a professional assassin and a mutant with a well-developed bloodlust. He and Wolverine are deadly enemies and well-matched: Sabretooth's psychotic tendencies are the perfect foil for Wolverine's berserker rages.

○ £ 4–6
○ $ 6–9

○ **£**18-22
○ **$**27-33

➡ *2000 AD* was launched in Britain in 1977 and soon attracted a huge following, which continues to this day, with fan clubs and conventions galore. It is Britain's answer to a question that was probably never asked. Its superb blend of black humour and wry irony are part of a winning formula that has enabled it to compete with the best American titles. The comic also revived Dan Dare in the 1970s, changing his style somewhat to suit that of the publication. This is a scarce issue from 1978.

⬅ Judge Dredd was undoubtedly *2000 AD*'s best-known character; this is issue number 1, volume 1 of Dredd's own *Magazine*, which appeared in 1990. As with many British comics, free gifts were and are often used to pull in new readers, and the first issue of volume 2 offered a free badge. Such gifts add to the collectibility of the comic and that issue is worth about £6/$9 with the badge, but only £3/$4.50 without. As a first issue, the comic shown here certainly has collector appeal. Its current value of around £5/$7.50 doesn't sound like a lot, but in percentage terms it has made big gains on its original cover price of £1.50.

○ **£**4-6
○ **$**6-9

○ **£**3-5
○ **$**4.50-7.50

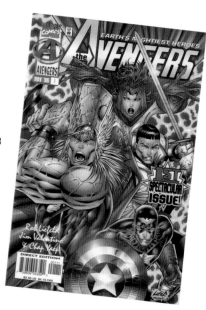

➡ The 1990s were difficult for the Marvel group, which became embroiled in financial wrangling and takeovers. Characters became samey and sales fell. One response was to produce a range of retrospective comics, repackaging familiar heroes for a new generation. The Avengers, a Silver Age crimefighting team, got the treatment. Ace artists Rob Liefield and Jim Valentino, who had left to form a new company, were among those given the job of revamping the titles. This is issue 1, volume 2, from 1996.

○ **£** 10–15
○ **$** 15–22

➥ *The X Files* as a TV series may be over, but the comic-book spin-offs are still very popular – some dealers report that they can't get enough of them, and the demand has naturally been pushing up prices. Pictured here is a special collector's issue. The show has such a strong following that it is hard to imagine that these comics won't continue to be sought-after for a long time to come. American Alex Saviuk and British artist Charlie Adlard were among the illustrators.

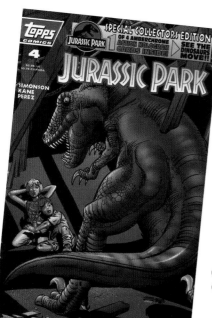

◀ Topps, the trading card firm, produced a series of comics during the 1990s before pulling out of the medium towards the end of the decade. This *Jurassic Park* comic, for the 1993 blockbuster movie, came in two versions, a general news-stand version and a "special collector's edition", seen here. The latter had cards inside – these were different from the cards produced separately for the movie and could add 50p–£1/75c–$1.50 to its value. Never very popular, the title had been discontinued by the time the third film came out in 2001.

○ **£** 1–2
○ **$** 1.50–3

○ **£** 8–10
○ **$** 12–15

➥ Tomb Raider is something of a legend among computer games and, although it's been a while now since it first appeared, anything to do with its heroine Lara Croft is still very popular and prices have been rising steadily. Produced by independent publisher Top Cow, the comic is particularly collectible – not only as a first issue, but also with the gold variant cover (publishers sometimes produce editions with different covers in the hope of attracting collectors, often with success, but fans do like the stories inside to be worth it). The writer of this 1999 issue is Dan Jurgens, who has written for such heroes as Superman and Thor.

Graphic Novels

Graphic novels are, as the name suggests, novels with graphics – essentially novels in a comic-strip format (although some are compilations of comic-book stories). The first ever graphic novel, *A Contract With God* by Will Eisner, was published in 1978. Marvel's first effort was *The Death of Captain Marvel*, published in 1982, and a first print of this title would be worth in the region of £20–30/$30–45 today. Graphic novels have numerous advantages over comics, not least because the book format makes them more durable. However, it's not just about durability: graphic novels also use the very best artists and writers, so sheer quality is certainly another consideration. They also offer value for money – you can get a really good, full-length story for the price of three or four comics. Graphic novels are mainly collected for the characters, and all of the major comic publishers produce them as they offer the writers the chance to develop and explore their characters in greater depth. The novels don't have to relate to the comics, so the storylines and characters have often been changed.

First published in 1988, *Batman – The Killing Joke* is considered quite a landmark in graphic novels. It tells us something of the origins of the Joker, Batman's most famous adversary, but it is also a dark tale exploring the complex relationship between hero and villain. It was penned by Alan Moore, who wrote *Watchmen*, an acknowledged classic in the genre. The artist was Brian Bolland, a stalwart of the *Batman* comics, who also worked on *2000 AD*. This is a first printing.

○ **£**18–22
○ **$**27–33

○ **£**18–22
○ **$**27–33

The sci-fi/horror movie *Alien* was famed for its graphic detail, so a graphic novel seems perfectly appropriate. Shown here is a rare first print of *Alien – The Illustrated Story*, by Archie Goodwin and Walter Simonson, which was based on the movie. Goodwin was a highly experienced and very successful comic-book writer, who worked for Harvey Comics and for Warren Publishing. Walter Simonson began his career as a freelance artist and drew characters such as Batman and the Hulk. After working on this novel he both wrote and drew *Thor* for Marvel Comics, and it was for this that he won the Haxtur Prize for best writer.

➡ *Swamp Thing* is a good example of how graphic-novel writers can be freed from the constraints of the comic storyline. It has been described as an "eco-horror", and was originally about the ghost of a man who refuses to accept death, creating a body for himself from the swamp. Swamp Thing moved on, accepting that he was no longer human but had become a monster, and writer Alan Moore's well-rounded characterization is a delight. The artwork by Steve Bissette and John Totleben is greatly admired by collectors, creating arguably the definitive version of the swamp. Shown here is the first printing, which is hard to find.

○ **£**13-17
○ **$**20-25

○ **£**8-12
○ **$**12-18

↑ The two "Conan" movies, starring Arnold Schwarzenegger, were both hits, but this graphic novel from 1990 is for a third film that was never actually made, and this adds interest in itself. Artists include the Philippino Tony DeZuniga, who worked on many Marvel and DC comics and introduced several other talented artists from his native country to these publishers. Writer Roy Thomas was chief editor at Marvel in the early '70s, writing and editing for all of their most famous characters.

🔽 Superheroes are always easy targets for parody, but the Teenage Mutant Ninja Turtles pushed it to the limits merely with their name. Kevin Eastman and Peter Laird created them, alluding to the "alligators in sewers" urban myth, as well as to mutant superteams such as the X-Men. The turtles' rise was meteoric, and by 1990 they seemed to be everywhere as the movie, which this novel accompanied, became one of the year's biggest box-office hits, grossing $135 million.

○ **£**8-12
○ **$**12-18

Manga

The word "manga" was coined as far back as 1815 by the famous Japanese woodblock artist Hokusai to describe his comic sketches. Literally meaning "involuntary pictures", today it is used to describe the uniquely Japanese style of comic book that is a major form of entertainment in that country – comics are not stigmatized as children's entertainment in Japan, and adult titles on many different themes abound. Manga now has a sizable and growing following among Westerners, who have come to appreciate the dynamism and ingenuity that characterize the genre. In recent years, the influence of manga on the American comics industry has been growing and no wonder, for Japan boasts the world's largest comics industry. Historically, that industry had many advantages over its American counterpart, not least because Japan did not suffer any "moral panics" over content, so the creative teams could explore a myriad of themes that allowed the medium to flourish. Manga has also had a strong influence on animation art. Manga is incredibly complex; it is rooted in a variety of artistic and cultural assumptions and values, and has been the subject of many a university thesis. Here are just a few examples of this fascinating and rewarding genre.

○ £2-4
○ $3-6

↑ Godzilla is not just a Japanese icon but also probably their best-known sci-fi and fantasy export. *Godzilla, King of the Monsters* had originally been published in black-and-white in 1987, but in 1998 it was back in colour, courtesy of publishers Dark Horse – this is the first issue. These publishers produced many English-language versions of *Godzilla* manga, and this story was by top Japanese writer Kazuhisa Iwata. It came at an appropriate time for Japan's favourite dinosaur to get another comic-book outing, for it was the year in which the blockbuster Hollywood film *Godzilla* was released.

○ £2-4
○ $3-6

← *Lone Wolf Cub* is an epic samurai adventure story and an acknowledged manga classic; the hugely popular series comprised more than 8,000 pages. Kazuo Koike's superb writing combined action and adventure with history to create this tale of a wandering renegade samurai and his son. The cinematic-style images of Goseki Kojima are reminiscent of the work of Akira Kurosawa. In the late 1980s, the now-defunct US publisher First Comics brought the saga to English-speaking audiences, and this is one of those early issues. The series has recently been revived by Dark Horse comics.

○ **£4-6**
○ **$6-9**

In 1979 Japanese manga publishing giant Kodansha agreed to fund an animated movie of E.E. "Doc" Smith's classic *Lensman* series, combining computer and cel animation, which finally came out in 1984. The stories lend themselves well to the comic-book format and, not surprisingly, they became a huge hit in this medium. This is the first issue of Eternity Comics' 1990 publication of the Japanese Lensman animation in English.

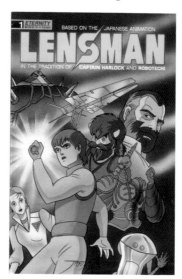

○ **£4-6**
○ **$6-9**

Only those who have been living on Mars for the past few years can have failed to notice Pokémon. Pokémon, or pocket monsters, started life in 1996 as characters created for the Nintendo Game Boy. TV shows and movies followed, and, of course, trading cards. Published by Wizard, this is a special-edition guide to Pokémon. The slogan "Gotta catch 'em all" was not just aimed at trading-card collectors but was also designed to make enthusiasts into "completists", so anything relevant is sought-after. A word of warning: Pokémon collectibles were made in large numbers!

The *Star Wars* movies achieved worldwide popularity, and were as loved by audiences in Japan as elsewhere. *Star Wars* got the manga treatment in a stunning

○ **£7-8**
○ **$10-12**

adaptation, published in 1999, which was beautifully illustrated by Shin-Ichi Hiromoto with cover art by Adam Warren. Pictured above is the concluding instalment of *The Return of the Jedi*. There is some crossover here, because this series will be collected by die-hard *Star Wars* fans as well as manga enthusiasts.

Toys

Toy collecting has been popular for a long time, but it has often been regarded by other collectors as rather an odd, or even childish, pursuit. However, as the field has developed and the big auction houses have taken an interest, so the realization has dawned that toy collecting is far from child's play. Many old toys are only suitable for adults, either because of their lead content or because of sharp edges, and nowadays all kinds of toys are made specifically for the adult collectors' market. However, many adults are trying to rebuild childhood collections for nostalgic reasons, and so prefer old toys. Sadly, rising prices have meant that there are many areas, such as early tinplate toys, in which good examples are hard to find or are too expensive for those of modest means. If you buy today's "must-have" toys and keep them in their original boxes, you might find you can sell them to a nostalgic thirty-something for a tidy profit in 20 years' time.

Toys

A recognizable toy market first began to take shape in the 19th century. The sign of an affluent society, it grew rapidly in the 20th century, especially post-World War II, with the influence of TV, movie, and scientific advancements. Fantasy and sci-fi have captured a huge share of the toy market and this looks set to continue. Given the enthusiasm of children, it is surprising that any older toys survive at all; in fact it is tempting to suppose that survivors were unwanted and never played with. Sometimes this is true, but some have simply come from homes where "after play, put away" was the family motto, so they have survived with their boxes and accessories. Boxed versions of any toy will always be more valuable, possibly worth several times as much as a loose example. This is partly because a boxed toy will have been better protected from environmental conditions, but also because packaging can tell you a lot about the toy itself. The boxes, too, should be in good condition to secure the best price.

○ **£** 40-60
○ **$** 60-90

⬆ Doctor Who had numerous companions but his robotic sidekick K-9 was the oddest of them all, joining the Doctor during his Tom Baker incarnation (1974–81). Many fans found him tiresome, but younger viewers loved him and Palitoy's talking version was a decent enough toy. It talked with the aid of a small disk, like a record, that could be turned over for more phrases.

○ **£** 50-80
○ **$** 75-120

⬆ The Daleks rate among the greatest sci-fi villains of all time, their evil demeanour overcoming their "pepperpot" appearance. Several toy versions were made, including 1960s battery-operated models by Marx that have reached £300/$450 at recent auctions, and this 1970s talking Palitoy version. It speaks several appropriate phrases, but, unlike K-9, its record has only one side and therefore a limited repertoire. Boxed versions sometimes turn up, but a damaged weapon or eyepiece will lower the price.

Steve Zodiac, hero of Gerry Anderson's *Fireball XL5*, is instantly recognizable as a Pelham puppet because of his bright pink face and distinctive look. Launched in 1947 by Bob Pelham, the firm also made puppets of a huge range of TV characters, from Andy Pandy to Brains from *Thunderbirds*, but finally went into receivership in 1992. Pelham's puppets are much admired by professional puppeteers, who appreciate their quality. Replicas have been made in recent years, but these are signed and dated to avoid confusion.

○ **£**150–200
○ **$**225–300

When *Batman* became a TV series in the 1960s it was a huge hit, and spawned a variety of toys. This inflatable walking Batman is among the more unusual, and was produced by the Louis Marx company in 1966. Inflatable toys of any kind are vulnerable to the rigours of play, and these toys are particularly rare, hence their "inflated" value today.

○ **£**280–300
○ **$**420–450

○ **£**50–60
○ **$**75–90

With the success of the *Batman* TV series every child wanted to be Batman, prompting safety concerns as children leapt from kitchen tables and worse. The luckiest among them were clad in this playsuit made by the Ideal company, who had several Batman lines. It was made in 1966, and it has to be said that it was a rather loose interpretation of the Caped Crusader's own outfit. Playsuits are clearly prone to wear and tear and are therefore quite rare survivors.

Tinplate toys were revolutionized in the 1880s by the development of lithographed tin. Colours and detail could be printed onto flat sheets of metal with a press, and the toys could then be formed with tools and dies. Tinplate toys are very collectible, and this "Atomic Rocket" spaceship, by Masudaya, is typical of the output of many Japanese firms of the 1950s. Its very title reflects the concerns of the time, atomic energy and space travel being in their infancy. Operating the lever on top of the ship provides the friction power to propel it forward.

○ £400-500
○ $600-750

Japanese manufacturers produced several different versions of tinplate flying saucers during the 1950s and 1960s; this example was made by Masudaya. Founded in 1924, Masudaya is still in business to this day, and usually brands its toys with an "MT" (for "Modern Toys") logo. This toy is battery-operated and has a "bump'n'go" mechanism, with sequential flashing lights around the edge of the saucer. A very similar saucer was made in the 1960s by another firm, but it has more yellow in its decoration around the rim, and is worth about two-thirds as much.

○ £125-175
○ $190-265

Major Matt Mason was an Action Man-type figure produced by Mattel from 1967 until the early 1970s – a fairly short period – and his decline in popularity perhaps reflects the loss of interest in and cancellation of the Apollo lunar exploration programme. This is his Space Crawler which, if it looks odd, is no stranger than some of the real-life designs on the drawing-board at the time. This battery-powered vehicle could clamber over most domestic obstacles, but the spokes and hubs are often damaged or missing today.

○ £100-120
○ $150-180

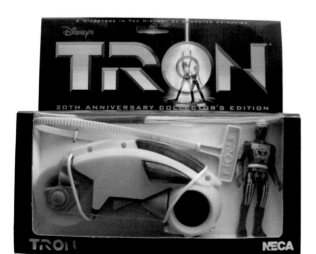

↑ Tracy Island is the secret base of the philanthropic Tracy family, who operate International Rescue in the *Thunderbirds* series. When the show was repeated in Britain in the early 1990s, manufacturers and retailers seriously underestimated the demand for this toy, and many children were disappointed as a result. The island, made by Vivid Imaginations, was battery-operated and had numerous sound effects; figures and vehicles were available separately. It had its critics, who felt it was a bit flimsy – especially the palm trees and swimming pool cover that did not always endure the rigours of play. If you have a survivor, you have a worthwhile collectible.

○ **£** 25-35
○ **$** 38-52

○ **£** 20-30
○ **$** 30-45

◀ The lightcycles were among the most memorable creations featured in Disney's groundbreaking movie *Tron*, released in 1982. They were reproduced by Tomy, but this is a later version, made by NECA for Tron's 20th anniversary. The company name is printed on the right side, so it cannot be confused with an original. Made in a limited edition of 5,000, they could prove a good investment.

○ **£** 15–25
○ **$** 22–38

➤ The AST 5 was one of a number of "mini-rigs", or smaller vehicles, that appeared in the *Star Wars* movies – this one is from *Return of the Jedi*. AST stands for Armoured Sentinel Transport, and the AST 5 is described in the original catalogue as "an awesome anti-gravity ship". Its role was to defend the base of the gangster Jabba the Hutt. As is typical of *Star Wars* toys, the packaging features pictures of the other vehicles in the series, in order to inspire children to collect them all. The AST 5 was first issued in 1983; the 1984 re-release shows only four vehicles on its packaging instead of the six shown on the original version here.

➡ The AT-AT (All Terrain Armoured Transport) is one of the most impressive of all the *Star Wars* toys. It provides perhaps the best demonstration of the idea that smaller action figures could be used with the toys. The AT-AT could hold two figures in its cockpit, and a further ten inside the main body. This one was made by Palitoy to accompany *The Empire Strikes Back* (1981), in which the AT-AT first appeared. They were expensive at the time so were made in smaller numbers. Hasbro made an AT-AT in the '90s using the same moulds, but numerous modifications were made to differentiate.

○ **£** 150–300
○ **$** 225–450

○ **£** 30–35
○ **$** 45–52

⬅ A repulsive, slug-like figure, Jabba the Hutt makes a memorable villain in *Return of the Jedi*. This playset, issued in 1983, shows Jabba with his minions, including his monkey-like pet, Salacious Crumb. It is not too hard to find without its box, although accessories, such as his hookah pipe, are often missing. It is easy to see why boxed examples of any item are highly valued, since it is more likely that such accessories will be present. The price guide given here is for an unpackaged figure – the boxed ones will sell for more.

The Millennium Falcon was, in many ways, the flagship of the *Star Wars* toys fleet. This replica of Han Solo's ship was issued in a variety of packaging including, as this example indicates, a version to tie in specifically with the third film, *Return of the Jedi*. Although many of these battery-operated toys were made, and they do appear on the market, they are rarely in mint condition. Throughout all the packaging changes the ship remained much the same, and it is important that the hatches and other gadgets work.

○ **£** 75–150
○ **$** 115–225

○ **£** 7–8
○ **$** 10–12

The Ewoks made their debut in *Return of the Jedi* and, while many adults had their reservations, kids loved them. In 1984 they hit the small screen with animated adventures, and this Ewok, based on the character Wicket (aka Wicket W. Warwick), is from the accompanying range of toys, which included elaborated playsets. Just 5cm/2in high, they were intended for small children.

○ **£** 150–200
○ **$** 225–300

Luke Skywalker's Land Speeder can be seen here in two versions: a British one by Palitoy (above) and an American version by Kenner (right). Both are from the original issue of these toys, the main difference being that the bonnet opens on the Kenner version but not on the Palitoy one. In 1979 the LP (Long Play) logo on the bottom right of the Kenner box was removed, so theoretically it is easy to recognize early boxed examples. The American version is worth less than the UK one, largely because many more were made; loose, unboxed examples are common.

○ **£** 65–90
○ **$** 100–135

Robots

No one can deny that the idea of using a mechanical person to carry out tasks on our behalf is very appealing. The use of the word "robot" to describe such an invention is credited to Karel Capek in his play *Rossum's Universal Robots* (1922), and is said to be derived from the Czech *robota* meaning "work". In the toy world, robots are often armed to the teeth, but can be friendly rather than aggressive. They are a post-war phenomenon, reflecting the promise of new technologies. Japanese manufacturers quickly dominated the field, producing numerous and varied designs. While many of them were developed as individual characters in their own right, comic strips, B-movies, and serials all provided inspiration. Condition, as always, is important, although even badly damaged robots are sometimes bought for spares. Robots should be kept away from dust, which can get into the mechanism, and damp – rust is a great enemy of tinplate examples. Remember that robots, like all machines, are happiest when working, so switching them on ever so often, even if briefly, will help prevent the motor from seizing up. Modern manufacturers are still making robots, sometimes as limited-edition collectibles, and these have proved popular with collectors.

○ **£** 700–1.000
○ **$** 1.050–1.500

Robby the Robot, from *Forbidden Planet* (1956), is one of the most famous robots of all time. He made further screen appearances in *The Invisible Boy* (1957), and he even had a cameo in an episode of *Mork and Mindy*. Several versions have been made, and modern-day replicas are still produced, but this 1950s battery-operated version in black tinplate by Nomura is the most desirable. This example was sold with its original box, which can more than double the price.

○ **£** 350–450
○ **$** 525–675

This Action Planet robot, made by Yoshiya of Japan, bears more than a passing resemblance to Robby. It is one of the last great tinplate and clockwork robots produced before plastic and battery-operation became the norm. Black is the usual colour for these toys, but a blue, battery-operated version was also made, as well as an extremely rare, olive-green wind-up version. "Warehouse finds" of these robots in the 1990s resulted in many of the common black versions coming onto the market, but because they are regarded as something of a classic they are always popular with collectors. This one came with its box, too.

The robot in the 1960s TV series *Lost in Space* was simply called "robot", but he is also labelled "B9 Environmental Robot" or "YM3" by Masudaya. Whatever his name, he was a major character in the show, with his big personality and distinctive design. Several toy versions were made. A 1960s version by Remco can fetch ten times more than this Trendmasters Inc. example, complete with box, made in 1997 – the year the story was set.

○ **£**30–40
○ **$**45–60

○ **£**18,000–25,000
○ **$**27,000–38,000

○ **£**3–5
○ **$**4.50–7.50

By the 1980s robots had become part of mainstream culture, and if they were not yet mowing the lawn and taking the dog for a walk, at least they could entertain us and tell us the time. These two, in the form of an alarm clock and a radio, were made by Tomy in the Far East. The radio robot "Mr. D.J." has moving arms, and dances to the music. Such robots are very much of their time and can still be bought quite cheaply, so they could prove to be a promising investment for the future.

This "Machine Man" robot is the rarest and most eagerly sought-after of the so-called "Gang of Five". These robots, which are battery powered, were made by Masudaya in the 1950s and are all similar in design, standing 38cm/15in high. The robot has "bump'n'go" action and flashing eyes, ears, and mouth. Masudaya made replicas of the "Gang of Five" in the late 1990s, but they are much smaller and so can be distinguished from originals. This 1958 example holds the world record auction price for a robot: it sold for a staggering $38,000 in New York in 2000.

The firm of Billiken made many robots, including this "National Kid". This tinplate wind-up robot was made in 1991, and is based on a character from a late 1950s/early 1960s Japanese TV show, *Leave it to Beibu*. This pioneering programme, featuring an alien superhero who comes to the aid of a group of youngsters, was credited with starting a boom in Japanese superhero shows. While Westerners may not be familiar with the show, an interest in Japanese popular culture in the West guarantees enthusiasm among Western collectors, as well as those in the Far East.

○ **£**80-100
○ **$**120-150

As toy robots have become more widely appreciated, many reproductions have appeared. While most are too obviously new to confuse anyone, with wear and time this could change, and of course they offer possibilities to the unscrupulous. One of the robots to be reproduced is this highly collectible astronaut known as Earth Man, originally made by Nomura of Japan in the late 1950s. Reproductions can be recognized by the inferior print quality of the face and the modern plastic parts of the battery-powered remote control. The copy should have a limited-edition number stamped into the inside of the foot; if this has been tampered with, the signs should still be evident.

○ **£**300-500
○ **$**450-675

The Micronauts were in many ways forerunners of the Transformers. They were interchangeable, so that parts from one could be added to another. Microtron was one of several slightly comical-looking Micronauts robots and, like Biotron below, was a good guy. He was battery-powered, and could be adapted to several configurations. Produced in 1976 he was one of the first, but he is by no means the hardest to find. A new range of Micronauts, including replicas of the originals, has been launched by Palisades, but these come in different shades to avoid confusion.

○ **£**15-25
○ **$**22-38

Originating in Japan, where they attracted a huge following, Micronaut figures, vehicles, and playsets were made for the West by Mego from 1976 to 1980, and were sold in the UK under the Airfix badge. Unfortunately, their joints could be a little flimsy. Their universe was divided into good and evil, and Biotron, the most powerful of the Micronauts, was one of the good guys.

○ **£**15-30
○ **$**22-45

○ **£**100-200
○ **$**150-300

Transformers were more than just robots in disguise – they became a phenomenon, and were the "must-have" toys of the 1980s. They were marketed by Hasbro and based on the shape-shifting robots of Japanese makers Takara. The Transformers' mythology centred on a battle between good Autobots and evil Decepticons. With their own TV show and comic they were a triumph of aggressive marketing, the like of which had not been seen before. This Decepticon Thrust was made in 1985 and comes complete with its original box.

For many collectors the wind-up tinplate robot is still king, and the golden age of toy robots ended when plastic and battery power became the norm. Still, plastic robots also have many fans, and some rare examples can sell for three-figure sums. This Eagleton Toys battery-operated robot, boxed, dates from the 1960s but is not particularly rare, hence its affordability. It is still possible to buy vintage tinplate robots at reasonable prices, but as they become more expensive and harder to obtain the alternative of plastic robots may become ever-more desirable. Plastic robots from the 1960s therefore represent a good opportunity for the future.

○ **£** 30-40
○ **$** 45-60

R2D2 ("Artoo Deetoo") from *Star Wars* is one of the most famous screen robots, and the popularity of the character and the huge international success of the movie led to several versions being made for different markets. This remote-controlled example by Harbert, in its original box, is from Italy where, it would seem from the packaging, he is known as C1P8. Presumably R2D2 doesn't quite work in Italian!

○ **£** 100-120
○ **$** 150-180

○ **£** 5-10
○ **$** 7.50-15

Like his partner, R2D2, the robot C3PO has inspired a huge range of toys and collectibles. This is actually a 1977 action figure rather than a robot, and a packaged first British issue can fetch up to £300/$450. There are also talking C3PO heads, figures, and clock radios for the recent movies. Limited-edition wind-up tinplate C3PO robots were made in 1997 by the Osaka Tin Toy Institute and sold for the same amount, but these were snapped up almost immediately.

○ **£**50-100
○ **$**75-150

The success of the *Robocop* movies inspired Billiken to produce this wind-up version for the third movie in the series. The litho and body pressing is well done and quite detailed, which makes for an accurate rendering of the character. The *Robocop* movies, like the *Alien* films, were quite violent and not really intended for children, but the video age meant that the kids were watching them anyway – and adults liked many of the toys, too.

○ **£**100-150
○ **$**150-225

These robots come from the Japanese TV show *Star Fleet*. It was a puppet show, with a storyline that revolved around the defence of Earth by heroes whose main hope lay in a new and powerful weapon known as the X-bomber. The programme featured the highly inventive kind of shape-changing robots that enthralled the Japanese public. *Star Fleet* was an excellent show and was shown worldwide, although it was sadly not as successful internationally as it deserved to be (possibly because of poor scheduling). The robots shown here were made for the Japanese market and are much sought-after by Western collectors.

○ **£**250-300
○ **$**375-450

Dolls

It is sometimes difficult to know where to draw the line between dolls and action figures. The smaller toys are clearly action figures, while the term "doll" is often used to refer to a larger figure that comes with clothes. However, what the lay person might consider a "doll" could equally be referred to as a "large action figure" – action-figure collectors tend to object to the suggestion that their objects of desire are "dolls", irrespective of their size! Even among collectors there is often a degree of overlap, and what is a "doll" to one is a "large action figure" to another. Most dolls come with accessories, which are easily lost in play; if they are missing, the toy will not achieve its maximum value. Several different versions of certain dolls exist and the keen collector will want to own as many as possible. In addition, most dolls were issued in different versions and packaging to suit the various international markets. Consequently, what is a relatively common doll in one country may be a sought-after rarity in another. Remember, if you have something you want to sell and are not being offered the right price, it might be worth trying the internet, in order to reach an international market.

- **£** 80-120
- **$** 120-180

⬆ Dolls based on the *Wonder Woman* characters have been around for many years, which is unsurprising given that the character dates from the 1940s. In the 1970s, a TV series starring Lynda Carter as Diana Prince/Wonder Woman introduced her to a new audience, and Mego responded with this Wonder Woman doll in 1978. The fully posable 30cm/12in doll made an appealing toy and came complete with a Diana outfit so you could dress her accordingly. It is now increasingly rare, and the accessories, such as her glasses, are often missing.

- **£** 50-80
- **$** 75-120

⬆ Action Man started life as Britain's answer to the popular GI Joe soldier dolls from the United States, and the first ones were produced in 1966. They overcame initial reservations from parents who were suspicious of "dolls for boys", and numerous versions were produced. While his soldiering was mostly earthbound, in the early 1980s Action Man did get to don a spacesuit to combat the alien menace in a largely unsuccessful attempt to repackage the hero for the *Star Wars* generation.

The *Thunderbirds* characters work very well as dolls, largely because they *are* essentially dolls – well, all right, marionettes – in the first place. In the 1960s, Fairylite made a number of *Thunderbirds* dolls, which can sell for as much as £150–200/$225–300 each today. In the early 1990s, the show enjoyed a revival with repeat screenings, which sparked a demand for toys from youngsters who were seeing it for the first time. Bandai of Japan made many toys, sold in Europe through Matchbox. Seen here are three of the five Tracy brothers by Bandai from 1992 – the price guide below is for a set of five.

○ **£** 200-250
○ **$** 300-375

○ **£** 30-60
○ **$** 45-90

This Tron doll is an extremely rare example, possibly the rarest *Tron* toy of them all. It was manufactured in the UK (and only in the UK) by Bendy Toys, and only a few were made. Therefore, as with the Bionic Woman doll (right), American collectors are particularly interested in him, although examples are rare even in Britain. There are no boxed versions because packaging was kept to a minimum: they were sold in a simple plastic bag. This was the only character from the movie to be made by the firm, and the moulds were apparently destroyed.

○ **£** 90-110
○ **$** 135-165

By the 1970s medical technology had made great advances, but not quite as great as those envisaged in *The Six Million Dollar Man* and its spin-off, *The Bionic Woman*. Jamie Sommers was the heroine of the latter, and Denys Fisher, under licence from Kenner, made this 30cm/12in doll. Two versions of the Jamie Sommers doll exist; in the first, she wears a white top and in this second version she has a blue outfit. This Denys Fisher version for the UK market is much rarer than the US Kenner version, so it is more desirable – especially to American collectors because it is particularly hard to find in the United States.

Games

There are fewer dedicated games collectors than there are collectors of action figures or trading cards, but sci-fi- and fantasy-related games do sell frequently at fairs and auctions. Because they are not always recognized for what they are, collectible board games still turn up at car boot (garage) sales. It is possible to spend a considerable amount of money on games but they are generally very affordable, and have still really not been "discovered" as mainstream collectibles. Factors that make them desirable include rarity, condition, and age – more or less in that order. All the relevant pieces should be there, and the box should be clean and undamaged in order for a game to fetch the best price. So many different games have been made that many collectors like to narrow the field by concentrating on specific makers, such as Parker Brothers or Waddington's; others prefer to choose a genre. Sci-fi-related board games make far more promising collectibles than other types of board game because they had a relatively limited shelf life. For example, Monopoly sets from the 1950s might be much less attractive to a collector than a space-related game from the '70s, simply because the latter would have dated more quickly and fewer would have been made.

○ **£** 10–15
○ **$** 15–22

⬆ Waddington's capitalized on the worldwide fascination with the real-life space programme by producing this Blast Off game, which appeared in 1969 – the year Neil Armstrong set foot on the moon. The game involved piloting spacecraft, making various manoeuvres, and landing on other worlds. Sadly, the gameplay let it down somewhat and it wasn't quite as exciting as it sounds.

○ **£** 1,000–1,300
○ **$** 1,500–1,950

⬅ If the movie *King Kong* had been made today it would have been accompanied by a vast array of products, as befits a film of such blockbuster status. But even in 1933 it had more promotional attention than a lot of its contemporaries, and a craze for jigsaw puzzles at that time encouraged this fine example of a then-popular marketing tool. This particular example is unique as it is the only one that is known to exist in near-mint condition, complete with its original envelope – hence its high value.

Dan Dare had a huge following from his very first appearance in the *Eagle* at the start of the 1950s. At the same time wartime restrictions and shortages eased and incomes grew, and games and toys based on popular characters began to fill the stores. This jigsaw has the advantage of being in its original packaging but the box, even though it appears to be unopened, has sustained some damage. It could therefore only manage £100/$150 when it sold at auction in 2001.

WADDINGTON'S
DAN DARE
JIG-SAW PUZZLE
DESIGN No 604
DAN AND THARL FIGHT IT OUT
OVER 200 PIECES · FULLY INTERLOCKING

○ **£** 100–50
○ **$** 150–225

THUNDERBIRDS 3D PAINTING SET

PAINTING BY NUMBERS (10 POSTER COLOURS)

The box makes it's own Picture Frame

THREE DIMENSIONAL! PAINT THIS FABULOUS PICTURE FROM THE EXCITING TV SERIES –THUNDERBIRDS!

MADE IN ENGLAND BY J. ROSENTHAL (TOYS) LTD.

The firm of J. Rosenthal made many *Thunderbirds* toys, including water pistols, vehicles, and this painting-by-numbers set from 1964. While it is not strictly speaking a game, it does illustrate many of the points that are common to such toys. All the pieces should be present, which in this case means the paints in particular. The box could be used to create a frame for your finished picture.

○ **£** 50–60
○ **$** 75–90

"Thunderbirds are GO!"

PETER PAN PLAYTHINGS LTD.
THUNDERBIRDS TO THE RESCUE
A TEST OF SKILL & CONCENTRATION FOR ALL AGES

For such a relatively hi-tech show in its day, *Thunderbirds* spawned some very traditional games, but the presence of the "FAB boys" guaranteed sales. This is perhaps the simplest of the *Thunderbirds* games made by Peter Pan Playthings, and involves getting balls into the right holes. The condition of both the box and its contents is, as always, important, and the balls must not be missing if it is to realize its maximum value.

○ **£** 60–100
○ **$** 90–150

○ **£**45-55
○ **$**68-82

🔼 This board game was made by Ideal and is based on the "Assault on MCP" (MCP being the Master Control Program) in the 1982 Disney movie *Tron*. In spite of the ground-breaking technology used in the movie, it was not a major commercial success; as a consequence, games such as this would not have sold well. This very fact makes these games more desirable today, and even an incomplete game might still sell for around £20/$30. A complete game, with all the pieces intact, including the cardboard MCP tower, would fetch around £50/$75.

○ **£**30-35
○ **$**45-52

🔼 The escape from the Death Star was one of the most exciting episodes in *Star Wars*, and this board game, made by Palitoy in 1977 for the British market, found its way into many a Christmas stocking in the late 1970s. Kenner made the US version, which is slightly less valuable. *Star Wars* toys from Britain and other countries are often rare in the USA, so they are particularly prized by American collectors. For this game Luke Skywalker's hair is modelled in a "slicked-back" style for the trash compactor scene.

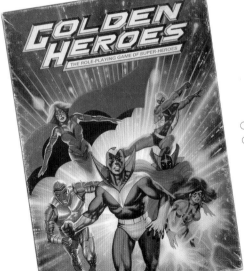

○ **£**20-25
○ **$**30-38

◀ Although popular in the 1970s, fantasy role-playing games underwent their real boom in the 1980s. The best known was probably Dungeons and Dragons, but there were many others. Firms such as Games Workshop not only sold but also made games, including Golden Heroes, which had a superhero theme. It wasn't particularly successful and was soon out of print; nevertheless it is much admired by aficionados of the genre – some regard it as the best superhero role-playing game of all.

The American company TSR introduced its Buck Rogers in the 25th Century role-playing game in 1990, based on the original comic strips rather than the TV series. The boxed set included colour maps of the various locations described in the game, as well as cards, counters, and dice. While some games required the purchase of several manuals and assorted items, here you had everything you needed to play "straight out of the box". This game has been out of print for some years and is becoming more difficult to find.

○ **£** 15–20
○ **$** 22–30

○ **£** 10–15
○ **$** 15–22

The Six Million Dollar Man and its spin-off, The Bionic Woman, were huge international hits, as were the associated games and toys. Although the bionic couple still have their fans, these are not among the most valuable of collectibles. However, there are rumours of a new movie, which, if it happens, could stimulate collector interest – so these items could prove to be good buys for the future.

○ **£** 1,500–2,000
○ **$** 2,250–3,000

○ **£** 15–18
○ **$** 22–27

The end of the 1970s saw the beginning of the micro-chip revolution, and with it came the arrival of the first electronic games (although many were too expensive to challenge more traditional games). This Star Wars X-Wing Aces game could perhaps be described as one of the "holy grails" of Star Wars collecting. It is an electronic target-shooting game made by Kenner in 1978, and is very rare today – hence its high value.

By the 1980s electronic games had spilled out of the arcades and into the home. This Tomytronic Sky Attack game by Tomy was one of six (with Sky Duel, Planet Zeon, Thundering Turbos, Jungle Fighter, and Shark Attack). They were similar in design, with different colours and labels on the casing. In many respects they are descendants of Victorian optical toys, and the forerunners of the Gameboy. As early examples of their type, especially if boxed, they may prove a good investment.

Die-cast Toys

Frank Hornby (of model railway fame) created the first Dinky toys in the 1930s, and such was their success that "Dinky" became almost a generic term for die-cast metal vehicles, regardless of who made them. For decades miniature versions of current cars and commercial vehicles were the norm, but sci-fi- and fantasy-based movies and TV shows gave the market a new impetus, and Dinky had the experience and expertise to produce a range of relevant toys. However, many die-hard Dinky enthusiasts frown on these toys, preferring models of real-life road vehicles. Collectors of more "conventional" Dinky toys are particularly keen on mint-condition examples still in their original boxes, and this is equally true of the TV- and movie-inspired range. Variations on conventional Dinky toys can also add considerably to their value. It could be that a model was produced in limited numbers as a prototype, or that a different colour was used, perhaps for an overseas market, along with a number of variations in styling. Toys based on specific vehicles "as seen on TV" would appear to have less scope for such variations, but they certainly do occur and, when found, they are snapped up by collectors.

○ **£**150-225
○ **$**225-340

SPECTRUM PURSUIT VEHICLE | 104

↑ The Spectrum Pursuit Vehicle (SPV) was one of the technological stars of *Captain Scarlet*. Die-cast toys made by Dinky soon became playground "must-haves", although they were quite expensive. The SPV came with a missile that could be fired from a hatch at the front of the vehicle. Such is the desirability of the 1960s Dinky 104 version that even in poor shape (missing tyres, damaged paintwork) it can fetch £20/$30 or so at fairs.

○ **£**140-190
○ **$**210-285

Dinky TOYS 105 | Maximum Security Vehicle **105**

↑ Also from *Captain Scarlet*, the Maximum Security Vehicle (MSV) was seen in far fewer episodes than the SPV. Its function, to provide protection for VIPs and transport precious or potentially hazardous cargo, made it less glamorous than the SPV, but it is still sought-after. Made by Dinky (No. 105 in the catalogue), it came with a "radioactive crate" inside but, like so many accessories of this type, this is usually missing. The example pictured here is an unusual variation in that its usually red interior is blue, which makes it more desirable. More common examples might fetch £40–50/$60–75 less.

➤ *UFO* may have been Gerry Anderson's first major live-action series, but real actors still failed to steal the limelight from the technology that was the hallmark of all his series. Armed with a single huge missile fitted with a nuclear warhead, interceptors (Dinky 351) were based on the moon and flew in packs of three as the first line of defence against the alien menace. The example shown here will be familiar to collectors, but a variation that had a black tip to the missile holder sold at a recent auction for £240/$360 – more than twice the expected amount for a standard version.

○ **£**90-130
○ **$**135-195

◀ If the aliens in *UFO* managed to make a landing on Earth, then mobiles could be deployed to attack them. These presented no major technical challenges to Dinky, which already had a range of tanks and armoured fighting vehicles – pre-production models used the wheels from a Leopard tank. There were two versions, one in olive green and the other in metallic blue. The blue version is less common and can fetch twice as much as the green version – one sold at a recent auction for £500/$750.

○ **£**250-350
○ **$**375-525

➤ Ed Straker was the head of the secret organization known as SHADO that protected Earth in *UFO*, and this is his car. The models were a little boring in comparison to the others in the same range – perhaps because Straker's car didn't have missiles. The car in the series did have gull wing doors, anticipating models such as the ill-fated DeLorean, but the Dinky 352 version had no opening doors. However, if you pushed the car backwards briefly then released it, it would propel itself forward a short way.

○ **£**100-150
○ **$**150-225

➡ The Batmobile was based on the Lincoln Futura, a concept car that appeared at the Detroit Motor Show in 1955. Its owner was commissioned to produce a vehicle for the new TV show in the mid-1960s and realized the Lincoln could easily be modified to fit the bill. Several manufacturers produced toy versions, including Husky and Corgi, who made this example. A version with red tyres was made, and these are rarer and more valuable than the black-tyred cars – a red-tyred Batmobile sold at auction in 2002 for £620/$930.

○ **£** 150–200
○ **$** 225–300

○ **£** 225–245
○ **$** 340–370

◀ Lady Penelope was International Rescue's glamorous London agent in *Thunderbirds*. Predictably, her pink Rolls-Royce was no ordinary status-symbol runabout and was well armed. Dinky No. 100, this vehicle featured figures of Lady Penelope and her trusty butler Parker, and fired a rocket from behind the radiator grille. It was in production for ten years from 1966.

○ **£** 100–150
○ **$** 150–225

➡ Joe 90, another Gerry Anderson creation, was a boy secret agent who could be given the brain patterns, and therefore the abilities, of just about anyone. His futuristic car, No. 102, was made by Dinky between 1969 and 1976 and featured opening wings and an extending tail – the independent suspension is also impressive. An example with a good, clean original box such as this will fetch a premium.

Thunderbird 2 was probably the most popular of all the *Thunderbirds* craft; its job was to carry vehicles and equipment to a rescue site. Dinky made a die-cast model (No. 101) from 1967 to 1973 and another, No. 106, from 1974 to 1979. No. 101 was made in green (the correct colour) and metallic blue, while the slightly larger 106 was blue. No. 101 is generally more desirable; a mint and boxed green example sold at auction for £340/$510 in 2002. A 106 may fetch only half or two-thirds as much as a 101. This early 1990s Matchbox model has thicker than legs than the original 1960s Dinky version, which is worth £180–250/$270–375.

○ **£** 10–15
○ **$** 15–22

○ **£** 70–100
○ **$** 105–150

Space 1999 was Gerry Anderson's second live-action series, first aired on British TV in 1975. The Eagle was the workhorse of Moonbase Alpha, where the story was set, and this Dinky Eagle came in two versions, a "transporter", soon followed by a "freighter". There was little difference, except that the transporter was green. They carried cylinders of "radioactive waste" with decals to apply to them – ideally, these should be unapplied. The freighters usually sell for slightly less.

Terrahawks was made in the 1980s, by which time Dinky was no longer in the market. However, the Japanese firm Bandai was just moving into the UK and produced a selection of six die-cast vehicles based on the show. A collection of all six sold at a recent auction for £100/$150. *Terrahawks* has not received the same attention as many other shows, but if it is revived these toys could well prove to be a good buy at their current prices.

○ **£** 10–20
○ **$** 15–30

○ **£**100-150
○ **$**150-225

↑ Corgi's range of Batman-related products reached new heights with their version of the Batcopter, which was originally based on a Bell military aircraft. It featured the attention to detail and working parts that were typical of the manufacturer. Corgi toys were not the cheapest on the market, but you got value for money – the Batcopter, for instance, has a working winch. The smaller "Corgi Juniors" version is also collectible, but it would fetch only about a quarter of the guide price quoted.

○ **£**250-300
○ **$**375-450

↑ This Corgi version of a Buck Rogers starfighter was made in 1979 and is a fairly realistic representation of Buck's ship, but with one important difference: the twin-boom design of the ship tapered to make two sharp points. These have been filled in with a strip of metal, presumably for safety reasons. It was made in two versions, the larger featuring opening wings and firing missiles, while the "Corgi Juniors" version just had opening wings. This is one of the larger ones and is a pre-production model, hence its value. More common "Corgi Juniors" versions sell for around £20/$30 or so, and the larger ones for two or three times that amount.

○ **£**100-150
○ **$**150-225

← Many different models of the *Star Trek* vessels have been made over the years, but few were as much fun as the Dinky die-cast versions issued in the late 1970s. This gift set pre-dates the first of the *Star Trek* movies, so the ships are modelled on those seen in the original TV series. The set comprised the USS *Enterprise* and a Klingon vessel, and offered great play-value as well as good models – the *Enterprise* fired plastic discs so that you could fight your own space battles.

○ **£**200-250
○ **$**300-375

If you think Black Beauty was a horse, then you're not a fan of *Green Hornet*, for this was also the name of that character's car. Typical of Corgi models, this vehicle offered a lot of play-value, with a missile to fire from the radiator, and a radar scanner that flew up out of the boot. Around three million of the original Corgi toy (No. 268) were sold, but they are hard to find today. Corgi have recently released a reproduction, but numerous minor differences, such as in the styling of the wheels, have been introduced to avoid confusion.

The Space Shuttle, first launched in 1981, promised easy and regular access to space – and naturally the toy and model makers were keen to get in on the act. Several manufacturers, including Corgi and Ertl, made some good-quality die-cast shuttles, while Dinky contributed with this version, which is quite rare today. The presence of unapplied decals adds to the value of this item; it is sad but true that the look of a toy can be ruined when decals have been applied clumsily, often by eager young fingers.

○ **£**100-150
○ **$**150-225

James Bond's adventures were usually earthbound, but he did get to board a space shuttle in *Moonraker* (1979). One of the original Corgi Moonraker shuttles made for the movie might fetch £50–90/$75–135, but this is a 1990s "Corgi Classics" version, so it would normally be worth rather less, perhaps £20/$30. However, this shuttle, which comes with a figure of Hugo Drax and a satellite, has been signed by Lois Chiles, who played Dr Holly Goodhead in the movie, hence its value. If you can persuade a celebrity to sign your collectibles, by all means do so!

○ **£**100-150
○ **$**150-225

Ray Guns

Toy ray guns were being manufactured as far back as the 1930s, to capitalize on the success of serials such as *Flash Gordon* and *Buck Rogers*. However, few of these have survived, largely because so many were melted down for their metal during World War II. The "golden age" of ray-gun manufacture came with the post-war era. Many different countries produced these toy weapons, including Britain, the United States, Italy, France, and Japan. Japan came to dominate the market, thanks to a combination of low costs and favourable trading agreements with the USA. What Japanese ray guns of the 1950s appeared to lack in quality, they made up for in sheer visual appeal and, of course, price. Those with sparking actions can be very attractive, but if the mechanisms are the worse for wear the value will be affected. It is not always easy to identify ray guns, and little has been written on the subject. Another point to remember is that popular designs were widely copied, so it is quite possible to find two virtually identical ray guns associated, by their packaging, with quite different characters. Some ray guns were not tied to any character.

While the box of this "Space Pilot Supersonic Gun" does not bear the name of Dan Dare, Britain's own space hero, a character resembling him does grace the front; some versions of his Planet Gun (pictured opposite) were not boxed as a Dan Dare toy either. Its beam is not a death ray but a simple torch, and the design is reminiscent of a 1950s Buck Rogers toy.

○ **£** 140-190
○ **$** 210-285

○ **£** 30-50
○ **$** 45-75

As with robots, some collectors prefer tinplate ray guns while others are happy to collect plastic versions. This plastic "Razer Ray Gun" was made by KO of Japan and is a good example of its type. Friction-powered, it has a sparking barrel and makes an explosive firing sound. While these guns are not that unusual or expensive, they appeal because they actually do something. Many collectors like their ray guns to be as lively as possible; some manufacturers even produced guns that emitted smoke!

○ **£**250-300
○ **$**375-450

➡ Several ray guns were made for Dan Dare, such as this "Planet Gun", made in 1953, and a "Rocket Gun" that fired rubber-tipped darts. You couldn't really shoot anyone with this gun, but instead it had three colourful discs that could be fired into the air. Dan Dare still has many followers, and new animated TV shows are bringing in more admirers. Fifties toys, such as this one, boxed and in good condition, are rare survivors. Its manufacturer, Merit, produced many toys, including a fine range of board games.

○ **£**400-500
○ **$**600-750

⬆ When the crew of Stingray had to leave the relative safety of their submarine, they protected themselves with weapons, although this gun looks unlike those featured in the series. It was made from a metal alloy by Lone Star, and was identical to a pistol they made for Dan Dare. Lone Star was a London firm – the name was chosen because of the popularity of Westerns when it began production.

⬇ Several different ray guns were made to accompany the ever-popular *Doctor Who* series, in spite of the fact that the Doctor himself was not noted for his gun-toting exploits. The Daleks stole the show, prompting a range of toys that didn't necessarily bear much relation to the series. This "Dalek Jet Immobiliser" – a fancy name for what was essentially a water pistol – was made in Hong Kong in 1965 and is a real rarity, hence its value. A "Fluid Neutraliser", made by Lincoln International in the same year, is also a water pistol!

○ **£**500-600
○ **$**750-900

Models & Replicas

Models, statues, and replicas have a large following, and each new series or movie brings with it new model kits, so there is always something new to collect. Many children "graduate" to models from more basic toys when they develop the skill and patience needed to put them together. Adults enjoy making and painting models, as well as statues or busts, of their heroes for display. It might seem that this is where the attraction lies, but a thriving resale market suggests that many people are prepared to pay for a well-made example. If there is one problem with models, it is that kits are more desirable in the resale market when they are unassembled – yet there seems little point in buying a kit if you are not going to use it. In recent years, many companies have begun producing replicas of items, particularly weapons, that appear in movies and television programmes. These are proving popular with fans, especially given the limited supply of actual quality props. Many replicas are made in only limited quantities, but it is still a little early to assess their long-term collectible value. As ever, much depends on the quality of the piece in question.

○ **£** 70-120
○ **$** 105-180

The Apollo moon landings inspired this Japanese lunar module. It lacks the detailed realism usually required of a model, and it is battery-operated so arguably it's really a toy. However, Tamiya made a fabulous kit (now rare) that was unquestionably a model, yet was motorized and had a propeller so that it could fly around a fixed point when attached to the ceiling. The lines between toy and model are less clear than is sometimes supposed.

○ **£** 40-70
○ **$** 60-105

Airfix is one of the best-known names in the world of models. The firm became famous for its quality range of plastic kits that, with glue, paint, transfers, and a little patience, could be transformed into models to be proud of. For many years, its most popular lines were aircraft from World War II, such as Messerschmits and Spitfires but, like Dinky, the firm took the opportunity to branch out with kits based on TV sci-fi shows. This example has not been assembled, which makes it more appealing to the collector.

○ **£**450-500
○ **$**675-750

The best replicas are those made with reference to original archive material, and supported by painstaking research. The American company Mr. Master uses such methods. Its products include this replica of Han Solo's blaster from *Star Wars*, which was based on German firearms used in World War II. This superb replica was made in a limited edition of just 1,500, all of which have been snapped up by collectors. Already expensive if you can find them, they look likely to hold their value as collectibles for the future.

Aurora, sadly no longer in business, is one of the most fondly remembered kit manufacturers; King Kong is a legendary fantasy icon. Put the two together and you have this fabulous glow-in-the-dark kit, made in the 1960s. As well as King Kong, The Mummy and Frankenstein's monster were also produced in this series. Aurora's kits are among the most desirable to collectors; this firm also made kits for series such as *Land of the Giants*, *The Invaders*, *Lost in Space*, and *Star Trek*.

○ **£**150-200
○ **$**225-300

Gerry Anderson's creations have always inspired model-makers, and renditions of his fabulous craft are not only sought-after by collectors but also used for promotion and advertising. This finely detailed replica of one of his early craft, Supercar, is a super car indeed. Made by expert model-maker Martin Bower, and more than 60cm/2ft long, it has a resin body with telescopic wings and a moulded perspex bubble canopy; hero Mike Mercury sits inside. The few surviving original Anderson models are extremely expensive, so replicas such as this make a more affordable alternative.

○ **£**2.000-3.000
○ **$**3.000-4.500

Trading Cards

Trading cards are popular because, at their best, they are works of art that can be carried around in the pocket. In recent years sci-fi and fantasy cards have become big business, and practically every series has cards associated with it. One method of attracting buyers involves "chase cards" – these are special "bonus" cards inserted at random into a very limited number of packs, so the chances of finding one are not high. They might be printed on a heavier card, or with a shiny foil finish, or they might be autographed by one of the stars. These autograph cards are naturally more desirable and, when found, they are sometimes removed from the packs and sold separately. Dealers sometimes assemble their own sets and offer them either as "basic" sets, or "complete" – that is, including chase cards. A recent trend has been the introduction of cards in a "wide-vision" format, which allows scenes from widescreen films to be shown more effectively.

TV Shows

TV shows offer plenty of opportunities to trading card manufacturers – the most popular programmes provide a large potential market for these products because die-hard fans will be added to the ranks of dedicated card collectors, snapping up anything to do with the show. As popular TV shows can run to a number of seasons, each new series heralds a fresh set of collectible cards picturing stills from different episodes. Spin-off series featuring popular characters can provide additional opportunities for card manufacturers and collectors. Someone once said that there is no such thing as a classic TV show, there are only cancelled shows. It's impossible to tell what effect the cancellation of a show will have on future prices, although, with endless repeat-showings and the devotion of fans, it's unlikely that today's TV hits will be forgotten for a long time to come. If axed shows are eventually revived, your card collection could attract renewed interest from collectors, but as always it's best to buy because you like the show, not because you hope to make money in the long term. All the price guides given here, and throughout the trading card section, are for complete basic sets, unless stated otherwise.

○ **£** 10–15
○ **$** 15–22

◀ The saga of *Buffy the Vampire Slayer* has been a huge international hit, spawning a variety of collectibles. These trading cards, made by Inkworks, are from Season Six, said by many fans to have been a milestone series in terms of plot development and excitement. "Piecework" cards randomly inserted into one in every 64 packs feature pieces of Buffy's top and Spike's T-shirt. A set of 72 Buffy cards from the first series can fetch as much as £40/$60.

○ **£** 10–15
○ **$** 15–22

▲ *Angel* is a spin-off from *Buffy the Vampire Slayer*, and it quickly established a cult following to rival that of its "parent". This first set, comprising 90 cards, was released by Inkworks in 2000, and chase cards included six autograph cards and special foil cards, the rarest of which is "Warrior's Destiny", inserted into one in 108 packs. This set makes a useful guide to the series because it includes character guides and a "demon's compendium".

"The Power of Three"

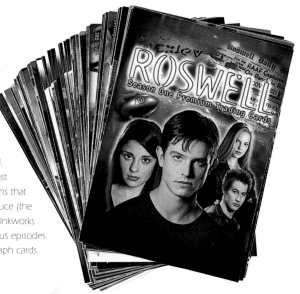

Like *Buffy the Vampire Slayer*, this sci-fi show, which features three glamorous witches, appeals to both sexes: female viewers enjoy the "girl power" and sisterly bonding of the main characters, while the attractive female leads guarantee male interest in the show. All this, and a supernatural fantasy theme too. These first-season cards were released by Inkworks as a set of 72. Bonus cards include cards that feature the "Book of Shadows", used by the Halliwell sisters to cast their spells.

○ £10–15
○ $15–22

Roswell is based on the mysterious events supposed to have occurred at Roswell, USA, where aliens and their craft were said to have been captured. The result is a show that combines sci-fi with teen angst. It was cancelled in 2002, in spite of a campaign by fans that included a mass mailing of small bottles of Tabasco sauce (the aliens' favourite). The main set of cards, first issued by Inkworks in 2000, features 90 cards picturing scenes from various episodes plus character profiles. Chase cards include six autograph cards.

○ £10–15
○ $15–22

○ £10–15
○ $15–22

Everyone's favourite sword-wielding amazon, *Xena* is New Zealand's greatest TV export. Set in a mythical past, the show makes compelling viewing. The cards aren't bad either; these cards for Season Six, the final series of the show, were released in December 2001 by Rittenhouse Archives, and there are 72 in a set. The print quality was much admired on their release, and both autograph and costume cards were issued. There is also a bonus card entitled "Forever Gabrielle", which contains a film cel.

KIRK AND KIRK

STAR SHIP ENTERPRISE

CORBY EXPLAINS

ANDROIDS ARE CALLED

MR. SPOCK

○ **£**600–800
○ **$**900–1,200

◀ While the recent *Star Trek* spin-offs have their followers, for many fans you just can't beat the original series – which is why Skybox released sets featuring Kirk and the crew in the 1990s. These sets are quite collectible and sell for around £10–15/$15–22, but here we see a set of original cards, which are worth considerably more. Released in 1969 with 55 in a set, they are really confectionery cards, because they were issued by A&BC and sold with bubble gum. If you have a set of these cards and they are in good condition, then you are sitting on something of a gold-mine.

"Space ● the final frontier"

○ **£**9–12
○ **$**14–18

➡ By the mid-1990s, when *Voyager* became the latest *Star Trek* spin-off, what was now being called a franchise had a loyal and established fan base. In the trading-card market, fans were catered for by Skybox, who issued this appealing set of cards for the first series in 1995. There were 98 cards in total, including 72 episode cards and 9 cards that assembled into a stunning picture. The set also featured cards offering a peek behind the scenes, and others that revealed details of 24th-century technology, or rather, how the ingenuity of the writers and special-effects people created it using the 20th-century technology available.

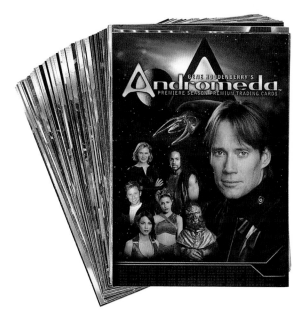

○ £9-12
○ $14-18

Andromeda was a long time in the making; Star Trek creator Gene Roddenberry had conceived the show long before his death in 1991, but his widow, Majel Barrett Roddenberry, took up the idea and it eventually aired for the first time in 2000. It stars Kevin Sorbo as the last starship captain of the System's Commonwealth High Guard, who is trying to save civilization from the chaos that followed a disastrous war. This 90-card set by Inkworks features episode cards and guides to alien races, while chase cards include foil puzzle cards, autograph cards, and costume cards.

The award-winning series Farscape tells the story of Crichton, an Earth astronaut. His ship has passed through a wormhole and he finds himself caught up in various adventures with a motley crew of shipmates aboard a living vessel. The show has now been cancelled, but further projects, including a movie, are possibilities. Released by Rittenhouse Archives in 2000, this set features 72 cards, three for each Season One episode. There are also "behind the scenes" cards, and preview cards for Season Two.

○ £9-12
○ $14-18

○ £10-15
○ $15-22

Babylon 5 was a remarkable series whose storyline featured political complexities, divided loyalties, romantic interest, and an almost Tolkienesque battle between good and evil. It had an international cast and also featured actors familiar to audiences from previous roles, such as Bruce Boxleitner (Tron), and Bill Mumy (Lost in Space). This set of cards, known as "Babylon 5 Profiles", was issued for the show by Skybox in 1999. There are 100 cards in the set, and they feature detailed profiles of all of the major characters from all five seasons. Chase cards include concept sketches for the alien make-up, and one very rare card detailing the career of sci-fi writer and B5 consultant Harlan Ellison.

Movies

Fantasy and science-fiction movie fans are especially devoted to their favourites, and the characters in them, so there is plenty of demand for associated merchandise such as trading cards. Packs that feature key scenes from the movie offer the chance for fans to relive classic cinematic moments at any time simply by reaching into their pockets. In the case of movies that run to a sequel, or several sequels, releases of trading cards may precede the release of the movie itself, giving collectors the chance of a "sneak preview". This has happened recently with both the *Harry Potter* and *Lord of the Rings* sequels. In return, the cards naturally help to promote the movie, and they guarantee that fans will be talking about it and eagerly anticipating its release, to the obvious benefit of box-office receipts. Such card releases do not have to spoil the fun for those planning to see the movie, whose plot may have been already widely and enthusiastically discussed and dissected on internet newsgroups before it is "in the can" anyway. It is also worth remembering that in the case of movies based on novels, such as *Lord of the Rings*, knowing the story does not ruin one's enjoyment of the production.

○ **£**8–12
○ **$**12–18

◀ The anniversary of a movie's release is as good a reason to issue trading cards as the release of a new movie itself. These cards are from a set of "Alien Legacy" cards, issued by Inkworks in 1999 to mark the 20th anniversary of the first *Alien* movie. As such, they are effectively commemorative items as well as trading cards. This 90-card set features scenes from all four *Alien* movies, plot and character details, and artwork and production information. The rarest chase card is entitled "Acid Bath", found in just one in 108 packs.

○ **£**8–12
○ **$**12–18

▲ Fifties-style alien-invasion films made a comeback with the hugely successful *Independence Day* (1996), which was visually stunning even if it did take itself far too seriously. Leading trading-card manufacturers Topps had the licence to produce cards, and rose to the challenge with a fine set of 72. They were produced in a "widescreen" format to give a more cinematic feel to the images produced, and this became a popular trend with manufacturers. A special "holofoil" chase card was inserted into one in nine packs.

○ £ 8-10
○ $ 12-15

THEY CAME FROM OUTER SPACE...
TO DESTROY OUR PLANET!

MARS ATTACKS!

WIDEVISION
MOVIE CARDS

THEY COME IN PEACE...

PLUS: DESTRUCT-O-RAMA
HOLO-FOIL CARDS!

PRESENTED IN

TOPPS
WIDEVISION

↑ *Mars Attacks* was originally a series
of trading cards issued more than 40 years ago.
In 1996, it was made into a movie by Tim Burton,
and Topps issued a new 72-card set to go with it.
The dark humour of *Mars Attacks* rang disappointingly
few tills at the box office in the United States, but
European audiences loved it. In many ways the movie
made the perfect antidote to *Independence Day*,
and the cards followed a similar "widevision" format.

🔖 The *Harry Potter* books were nothing less than a publishing
phenomenon, so it came as no surprise when the first movie was
such a big hit. Perhaps one day we will have the technology to
create cards like those collected by the Hogwarts schoolchildren.
In the meantime these cards, made for the first movie, were
produced by Wizards of the Coast, who brought
Pokémon to the West. There are
81 cards, including an index card.

○ £ 12-18
○ $ 18-22

"One ring to rule them all"

➡ *Lord of the Rings* was brought to life in spectacular style by
director Peter Jackson, and Topps produced cards to match, printed
on a suitably heavy card stock. This 90-card set is from the first movie
in the trilogy, and includes "behind the scenes" cards, character profiles,
and scenes from the movie. There are ten different "prismatic foil" cards and
no fewer than 13 different autograph cards. Like the movie itself, the trading
card sets are designed as a trilogy.

○ £ 12-15
○ $ 18-22

Miscellaneous

The sci-fi and fantasy market contains many "cross-overs" as comic strips are made into movies, movies become TV series, and TV series become comic books. Here is a selection of miscellaneous trading cards for various shows and movies. All kinds of subjects have been featured on entertainment-related trading cards, from comedy to horror, but sci-fi and fantasy lead the field. Trading cards have been produced for many years and movie stars were popular subjects for cigarette-card manufacturers back in the 1930s. Cards were of course given away with other products, from tea to bubblegum, and sporting subjects were very popular, as they still are. However, with the growth of the sci-fi and fantasy market, it is probably true to say that this genre now rivals sports cards in popularity. Of course, collecting has its fads and fashions, and you can never tell what will be popular in the future. For this reason, buy what you like – if you love the characters, then you will still love them whether or not your cards are worth more than you paid for them.

◀ Wolverine, Cyclops, Storm, and other members of the X-Men team were brought to life on the big screen in 2000, and in a set of trading cards by Topps in the same year. There are 72 cards in this set, and chase cards to look out for are ten different double-sided chromium finish cards, autograph cards, and "piece of the action" cards. The latter feature pieces of costumes used in the movie. With the arrival of a second *X-Men* movie, and the possibility of more to come in the future, the first cards are certainly worth collecting.

○ £8–12
○ $12–18

➡ Godzilla, one of Japan's greatest exports, has featured in movies, TV cartoon series, comic books, graphic novels, and a stack of merchandise since he was created by Toho in the 1950s. In 1998 he got the Hollywood treatment, and this set of cards, produced by Inkworks, was made for the movie. There are 72 cards in a set, including cards showing the artists at work creating the look of the monster for the big screen. Glow-in-the-dark chase cards, inserted into 1 in 17 packs, are a nice touch.

○ £8–12
○ $12–18

○ **£** 9-10
○ **$** 14-15

➡️ *The X Files*
gripped TV audiences
from its debut in 1993 and went on to
feature in comics, graphic novels, and, in 1998, on the
silver screen. These cards by Topps are for the movie.
The Australian firm Intrepid also made cards for the TV
series, but has since ceased trading, so this could add
to their cards' investment potential. This 72-card Topps
set was well regarded; chase cards included a set that
required warming in the hands to reveal the picture.

Stargate SG1 is the even more successful TV series
that was spawned from a successful movie. This 72-
card set, by Rittenhouse Archives, is from the fourth
season and has proved very popular with collectors,
so that they are already becoming hard to find. Some
cards are rarer than others; one such is a costume
card of Major Carter, which was thought to be made
in fewer quantities because of production problems.
This can sell for £100/$150, or even £200/$300.

○ **£** 13-15
○ **$** 20-22

○ **£** 8-12
○ **$** 12-18

◀️ This set of 66 cards was released for *Tron* in
1982 and was made by the Donruss Company.
Donruss is one of the oldest card companies
and specializes in sports cards. These *Tron* cards
are not very hard to find, but they must have
a set of stickers with them to make the set
complete. There were plans by the National
Entertainment Collectibles Association, who
released limited-edition *Tron* merchandise, to
re-release this set of cards, but nothing came
of it. The backs can be pieced together,
jigsaw-style, to form a picture, as seen here.

Bubblegum & Confectionery Cards

Today people buy trading cards, but they were once given away with confectionery. No-one was really fooled – we all really wanted the cards, and the bubblegum was just a bonus. Because they had to be collected gradually, and swapped with friends to obtain a set, perhaps only these can be considered true "trading" cards. The quality of the artwork sometimes varies, but they have great historical interest. This particular field of card collecting is often called "cartophily", a definition that originally applied to cigarette-card collecting. However, card collectors have long since branched out into cards that were given away with various products, known as "trade cards". Cards are graded according to condition, on a scale ranging from "mint" (perfect) to "poor" (major creases and/or tears), with six levels inbetween. Most dealers use much the same system and will be happy to explain it in full to the novice buyer. Cards should be stored away from bright light, and really valuable cards put in albums with Mylar sleeves. (Mylar is an inert material so there is less danger of damage from chemical reaction.)

○ £50-70
○ $75-105

↑ *Stingray* didn't just have a futuristic submarine, it had romance too. Here we see Atlanta (top left), Marina, and Troy Tempest (left), who formed a romantic triangle in the show. Also pictured here is arch-villain Titan, ruler of one of the underwater peoples. These cards were issued in 1964 and came in sets of 50. They were given away by the Primrose confectionery company of Slough with their packets of "sweet cigarettes", a type of confectionery that eventually disappeared from stores as they were seen to encourage smoking among children.

○ £50-75
○ $75-105

↑ Primrose also produced sweets and cards for other shows, including *Joe 90* in 1968. Like the *Stingray* cards, they came in sets of 50, but instead of artists' illustrations of the characters they used photographs. The back of the pack featured a W.I.N. (World Intelligence Network) badge to cut out.

Tazos are small discs that carry pictures of scenes from movies, in this case *Star Wars*. They have slots in them that allow them to be fitted together to play a game. They were included in packets of Walkers crisps and Doritos in 1997 in the UK, but not in every packet, so collecting them wasn't easy. If you found this too frustrating, you could order your missing tazos direct from the crisp manufacturer. Variations do exist – for example, on some discs the Biker Scout is labelled "Scout Trooper" – and these make them more desirable. Although individual discs are not worth much at the moment, complete sets are collectible and could fetch more in the future.

○ £10–15
○ $15–22

In the 1960s Adam West was the man behind the cowl in a tongue-in-cheek TV series that gave a new twist to Batman's traditionally dark comic-book character. These bubblegum cards were issued in the United States in 1966, and you would have had to chomp your way through at least 55 sticks of gum to obtain a full set. Complete, well-preserved sets from this era, in good condition, are quite rare, and this is reflected in the price.

○ £400–600
○ $600–900

Land of the Giants was a gripping 1960s sci-fi series by Irwin Allen (who also gave us *Lost in Space*, *Time Tunnel*, and *Voyage to the Bottom of the Sea*). This complete set of 55 bubblegum cards from 1968 is in excellent condition, hence the price. Be wary if buying over the internet: "mint condition" should mean perfect, and many would only apply this term to items that are in their original (also perfectly clean and undamaged) packaging. Make sure you are both talking about the same thing before you buy.

○ £400–600
○ $600–900

COMING TO SAVE THE WORLD
THIS SUMMER.

Movie Posters

Movie posters were originally produced for one purpose only: to advertise movies. Advertising art was widely ignored during most of the 20th century, and has only gained respect as art in its own right in recent decades. Posters were usually discarded after use, so surviving examples can be valuable. There have always been collectors, but until recently theirs was a minor hobby. Today "headline" auction prices have attracted media attention, which has in turn encouraged more collectors. Such is the popularity of science-fiction and fantasy that prices for this genre are escalating. There is a lot of material around, but there is also a great number of collectors chasing it. Collectors look for many things, including unusual variations. Many different versions were often produced for the same movie, and foreign-language posters of English-language movies are always interesting. However, it is a striking image that will always sell a poster – just as it sold the original movie.

Movie Posters

Science-fiction and fantasy are currently very big among dedicated poster collectors, particularly the sci-fi films of the 1950s. Horror is also popular, and there are many movies that blur the lines between the two genres, *The Thing* being an obvious example. It is perhaps not surprising that sci-fi and fantasy posters are so popular, because by their very nature they can offer the kind of stunning, imaginative images that show off the medium to its best effect. These posters are more than just works of art; like the films they advertise, they reflect the concerns of their time rather than just providing escapist fantasy. Examples of this include the "alien invasion" films of the McCarthy era, and the optimism of *2001: A Space Odyssey*, made when the Apollo space programme was well underway. If you want to collect movie posters, or simply gain a better understanding of them, then it is a good idea to make a habit of attending auction previews and poster galleries. It will cost you nothing, and you will really be able to get a "feel" for a genuine vintage poster.

○ **£** 50-75
○ **$** 75-115

○ **£** 30-50
○ **$** 45-75

🔼 Fritz Lang's *Metropolis* is one of the greatest sci-fi movies of all time. This German cinema classic was made in 1926 and set in 2000, which was then a lifetime in the future. The Italian poster above is for Giorgio Moroder's 1984 re-release. With its new soundtrack, tinted sequences, and shorter running-time (83 minutes), the movie offended many aficionados. Also shown here is a double-sided UK poster for the 2002 re-release, which featured an orchestral score. Both bear a striking image of Maria, one of the most impressive robots ever to grace the silver screen.

Alex Raymond's comic-strip hero Flash Gordon spawned three hugely successful serials: *Flash Gordon* (1936), *Flash Gordon's Trip to Mars* (1938), and *Flash Gordon Conquers the Universe* (1940), not to mention a camp re-make in 1980. Its combination of kitsch sets, corny dialogue, and a hissable villain (Ming the Merciless) guaranteed that Flash Gordon would never be forgotten. This one-sheet is for a 1947 re-release. It is desirable in itself, but a one-sheet for the first movie is worth considerably more, and can sell for as much as £35,000/$52,500.

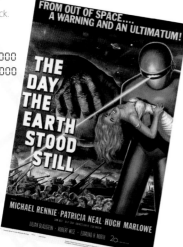

○ **£** 325-400
○ **$** 490-600

○ **£** 525-675
○ **$** 790-1,015

"Keep watching the skies" warned the poster for *The Thing from Another World*, but this one-sheet offers no clue as to what we are looking for. The scary typeface reflects the intrigue surrounding this classic, which features a polar base under threat from an unknown creature wisely not shown too soon in the film. The 1982 re-make showed rather too much for some movie-goers! The real intrigue surrounded rumours of Orson Welles' involvement in the production.

Having seen the poster, people were surprised to discover that *The Day the Earth Stood Still* was an intelligent film with an anti-war message, which added a refreshing twist to the 1950s "alien invasion" movies. "Klaatu barada nikto", an order given to Gort the minimalist robot, has become something of a catchphrase among fans. This famous image has been reproduced countless times, and there are precise facsimiles on the market. Giveaways include a slight blurring of the image compared to the crispness of the original, and the whiteness of the paper on the back.

○ **£** 2,700-4,000
○ **$** 4,000-6,000

○ **£** 2,000-2,500
○ **$** 3,000-3,750

Invasion of the Saucer Men (1957), aka *Invasion of the Hell Creatures*, is great fun, and perhaps the ultimate B.E.M. ("Bug-Eyed Monster") film. This 68 x 107cm/27 x 42in US one-sheet is without doubt the ultimate B.E.M. movie poster. The "creeping horror from the depths of time and space" turns out to be the fabled little green men who land on Earth and meet their nemesis in the form of a group of teenagers. The monsters were menacing indeed, with cabbage-heads and needles that sprang from their fingers.

○ **£**275-325
○ **$**415-490

◀ *The Creature from the Black Lagoon* is one of many movies that blur the line between sci-fi/fantasy and horror. Originally made in 1954, in 3-D and with superb underwater photography, it is regarded as a classic, and was successful enough at the time to spawn two sequels. This French version of the poster is the petite; the grande version has different artwork, as do the many versions created by artists in the various countries in which it was released. Foreign-language posters represent the collector's best chance to acquire this title, because the original American posters can sell for £5,000/$7,500 or more.

○ **£**350-450
○ **$**525-675

➡ *The Incredible Shrinking Man* (1957) is the tale of a man who finds himself in reduced circumstances after encountering a radioactive mist. Radioactivity, it seems, could be responsible for anything in the 1950s. While this was a low-budget movie, the effects were reasonable enough – everyone remembers the hero's battle with the spider! Several images were produced for this movie, but this British quad (70 x 60cm/40 x 30in) poster is particularly collectible. It is certainly the rarest for this title, and is generally considered to be the best.

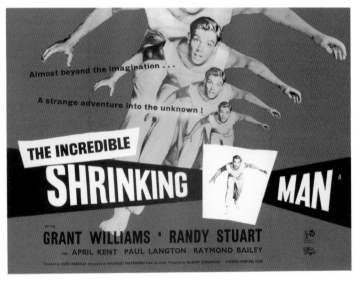

◀ *This Island Earth* (1955) has been described as "a science-fiction mystery". It is an intelligent film, and the bug-eyed monster only puts in an appearance towards the end. Nonetheless, it would be unthinkable at this time for him to be left out of the poster. This is a 104 x 68cm/41 x 27in US one-sheet poster, which has been increasing in value in recent years; ten years ago this poster was included at a Christie's sale with a £400–600/$600–900 estimate.

○ **£**800-950
○ **$**1,200-1,425

○ **£**550-650
○ **$**825-975

➥ *World Without End* (1956) was the first science-fiction movie to be made in Cinemascope, the cinema industry's secret weapon intended to combat the growing trend toward staying at home and watching TV. Sci-fi and fantasy were certainly well-suited to widescreen formats. This movie suffers from being overshadowed by better-remembered movies, such as *This Island Earth*, but it still has its followers, and the fact that it was something of a cinematic first helps to fuel collector interest. This is a US six-sheet 206 x 206cm/81 x 81in poster, whose image perfectly captures the movie's time-travel theme.

➥ Based on a Ray Bradbury tale, *Fahrenheit 451* tells of a future fascist anti-intellectual state in which burning books is part of a fireman's job. Directed by Francois Truffaut, and with an injection of glamour from Julie Christie, the 1966 movie of the book should have had a lot going for it, but critics considered it drab. The same could not be said for this French grande poster, which captures the chilling nature of the plot's premise. This poster, with artwork by Guy Gerard Noel, is considered far superior to the Hollywood version.

○ **£**400-525
○ **$**600-790

➥ Godzilla is Japan's greatest contribution to the sci-fi/fantasy genre. The resilient dinosaur is a national hero, and regular TV screenings of his movies, cartoon series, and a Hollywood blockbuster have kept the name alive worldwide. Here are two contrasting images, for an Italian release of the original 1955 movie, and for a Polish poster for *Godzilla versus the Smog Monster* (1971). Italian posters are usually direct and dramatic, while the stylized and highly intriguing graphics seen in the Polish example typify Eastern European art in the Cold War era.

○ **£**800-1,000
○ **$**1,200-1,500

○ **£**100-125
○ **$**150-190

There were many stunning images in *2001 – A Space Odyssey*, but only two were widely used in promoting the movie. One was the "wheel" space station, and the other featured astronauts on the lunar surface. For its Polish release, the then state-run distributors insisted on using their own designers, who interpreted the film in their own way, creating an interesting if barely recognizable *2001* image. The results are highly unusual and quite collectible. This wheel poster is a "lenticular" poster, made with plastic and designed to create a 3-D image when light shines through it – fewer than 20 are known to exist in this 58 x 84cm/23 x 33in version.

- ○ **£**2,675–3,325
- ○ **$**4,015–5,000

- ○ **£**525–675
- ○ **$**790–1,015

- ○ **£**530–670
- ○ **$**795–1,000

The original *Planet of the Apes* film, made in 1968, was based on a novel by Pierre Boulle. In many ways it is a brilliant satire reminiscent of Jonathan Swift, as well as a great sci-fi movie, although it is easy to forget how shocking the twist at the end really is when seen for the first time. This French grande (120 x 160cm/47 x 63in) is an example of a foreign-language poster that presents a different image from those used in English-language versions. These French posters were usually printed on fairly heavy paper and folded.

David Bowie lent his otherworldly persona to the part of an alien in this 1976 movie, which is now a cult classic. Many critics thought it pretentious, but technically it was superb. This poster was among many commissioned by US arthouse cinema pioneer Donald Rugoff for his New York showings. The style of this poster is known as "Cinema One Negative", and there are some examples still in circulation.

- ○ **£**125–200
- ○ **$**190–300

The runaway success of *Star Wars* prompted all the major studios to start looking for a *Star Wars* of their own. Paramount found what they were looking for in the form of a show that had an established following and had been running on TV stations around the world for many years. That show was *Star Trek*, and the first of six movies starring the original cast premiered in 1979. This half-sheet poster, by the prolific artist Robert Peak, presents a bold and memorable image that is typical of his work.

○ **£**40–55
○ **$**60–82

○ **£**275–325
○ **$**415–490

Australia has a small but perfectly formed movie industry, and, as *Mad Max* showed, one that is capable of generating massive international hits to rival Hollywood. The sequels may have become increasingly silly, as they so often do, but the theme of futuristic highway wars over fuel struck a chord with audiences worldwide. Here is a 100 x 152cm/40 x 60in poster for the second picture: *The Road Warrior* is the US title for *Mad Max 2*, the movie that really secured success for the series in the USA. The larger, more dramatic format enhances this poster's collector appeal.

○ **£**65–125
○ **$**100–190

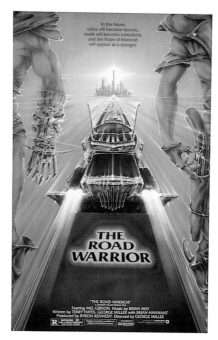

Star Wars is sometimes credited not only with reviving the sci-fi genre, but also with creating modern poster collecting as we know it. Certainly, it has come a long way from the small band of enthusiasts that used to categorize this branch of collecting, and *Star Wars* has helped to spawn some visually striking posters, and generated eager legions of potential buyers. This 1977 one-sheet poster is one of the best-known images, produced for the opening campaign. It came in a wide range of sizes, which helps to dispel the popular myth that Twentieth Century-Fox had little faith in the movie and hardly bothered to promote it.

○ **£** 650-750
○ **$** 975-1,125

◀ By the 1980s attitudes towards aliens were quite different from those of the 1950s. *E.T. – The Extraterrestrial* (1982) was a huge box-office smash as its family-friendly tale, in which the authorities, not the aliens, are the real villains, charmed audiences worldwide. The "flying bicycles" scene is one of the best-remembered from the movie, but this one-sheet image was withdrawn in favour of the "Creation of Adam"-style poster featuring E.T. reaching out to Eliot. The more familiar image is worth considerably less than the one shown here, and might only sell for £50–60/$75–90.

○ **£** 100-115
○ **$** 150-175

○ **£** 400-525
○ **$** 600-790

➡ Action, romance, metaphysics, and a haunting soundtrack – *Blade Runner*, based (loosely) on a story by Philip K. Dick, boasts all of these and more. The movie has great style; its advertisement-laden cityscapes have been copied, although never bettered, by many movies since. It is not surprising then that it has such a devoted following, and any original *Blade Runner* material is collectible. This image is the best known, but there is also a 20th-anniversary edition featuring Rutger Hauer, and a 1992 Director's Cut version (when the movie was released without the Philip Marlowe-style narration). Neither is as valuable.

▲ *Ghostbusters* is a highly inventive film, with great comic moments and an original premise. Interest in this engaging slice of fantasy was maintained for months before it was released by a series of "teasers" simply showing the "no ghosts" logo, and a promise that something was coming "to save the world this summer". Small ads even appeared in newspapers showing the logo and nothing else. This American poster finally revealed all. The poster is a one-sheet – during the 1980s this became standard, and almost all other formats were dropped.

THE DIRECTOR OF "BATMAN" & "BEETLEJUICE" INVITES YOU TO MEET HIS NEWEST CREATION:

edward
SCISSORHANDS

○ **£**65–85
○ **$**100–130

◀ *Edward Scissorhands* is an extraordinary movie, much more than the kitsch take on the Frankenstein story that some critics assumed it to be. Its darkly comic style is typical of the work of director Tim Burton but, like the eponymous hero, the movie was misunderstood when it was released in 1990, and enjoyed only moderate success. Since then it has attracted a cult following fuelled by word of mouth and its video release, hence the elevated value of this advance one-sheet poster. It is certainly a striking image, capturing perfectly the mood of the movie and its tormented hero.

○ **£**250–350
○ **$**375–525

○ **£**30–45
○ **$**45–70

➤ Getting the marketing right is an essential part of film-production these days, but there can be many unexpected obstacles along the way. Not one, but two posters for the blockbuster *Spiderman* movie, released in 2002, had to be withdrawn. The "teaser" poster on the right was produced in very limited numbers before falling foul of new US copyright laws – buildings can now be registered as trademarks, and the studio did not have permission to use the image of the Chrysler building, visible at the bottom left of the poster. Its replacement had to be withdrawn after the events of 11 September 2001 because the World Trade Center was still reflected in Spidey's goggles. The poster above left was finally released, but it is not nearly as valuable as either of the withdrawn versions.

Licensed Products

Some hobbies are collector driven and some are dealer driven, and movie posters are definitely the latter. One of the advantages held by dealers is the arcane jargon used to designate various sizes and formats of film paper. The following pages are an attempt to translate the more important terms into plain English. The history of movie-poster collecting is not only a history of film, but a history of paper and printing. Oceans of movie advertising were created during the 20th century and, while only a small fraction survived, it is still a large enough amount to support an active collecting obsolete. But they represent a rich history of promotion and exploitation, which helped build an industry founded on a fragile marriage of greed and dreams and has inspired a whole new created throughout the book when an interesting variation

Videos & DVDs

It is easy to forget that not that long ago, the only way of seeing your favourite shows again was by relying on the whims of the TV schedulers or an enlightened screening policy at your local fleapit. These days, of course, most homes contain an extensive library of movies and TV shows to be enjoyed at any time. The first domestic video recorders appeared in the shops in the late 1970s, so video cassettes have been around for a long time. As with records, there is a thriving market for videos, especially ones that are no longer available. Videos, also like records, deteriorate with wear. For the really finicky, "mint" condition means shrink wrapped – but most people like to *watch* their videos. While this is still a developing market, enthusiasts acknowledge degrees of condition between mint, or near-mint, and poor (in which the tape may not play properly and the packaging may be severely damaged or missing). DVDs now offer unprecedented choice to the viewer, who can decide not only what to watch, but also how to watch it. This growing market also offers various incentives to the collector via limited-edition packaging and special offers.

◄ *Doctor Who* was first made in the days when programmes were not always kept on tape for posterity, so many early episodes are not available, even to the BBC. "The Crusade" and "The Space Museum", featuring the first doctor, William Hartnell, were released in this two-video boxed set. This is a nice collector's package, which includes an audio CD for two missing episodes of "The Crusade", some limited-edition postcards, and a Tardis keyring.

○ £15–20
○ $22–30

○ £7–12
○ $10–18

▲ As with most collectibles, the value of a video will depend not only on how rare it is, but also on whether or not anyone wants to acquire it. Even the rarest of videos will not find a buyer if no-one cares for the title. However, *Tron* has a dedicated following and, like all true fans, *Tron* enthusiasts will want to own every version they can get their hands on. *Tron* was originally released on video in three variants: the regular retail version and two rental versions. Pictured here is one of the rental versions of the movie.

○ **£**20-40
○ **$**30-60

The *Tron* archive collection on laserdisc is perhaps the ultimate release of this movie. It is well packaged with attractive artwork, and includes an audio commentary by the director and production staff, together with all kinds of extras such as production sketches, deleted scenes and music, six different trailers, and storyboards. It also includes the original theatrical trailer, computer-animation demo reels, and more. Consequently, this is a valuable source of information as well as providing a copy of the movie. It is certainly a desirable addition to the collection of any *Tron* fan.

○ **£**80-120
○ **$**120-180

In *Tomorrow Never Dies* (1997), Pierce Brosnan as James Bond tries to stop a megalomaniac media tycoon, played by Jonathan Pryce, from starting a war in order to sell more newspapers. This special edition of the video was limited to 5,000 copies worldwide, and offers good value because you get not only the video but also a small camera (ideal for your own spot of espionage, perhaps) and an FM radio. It is also worth buying for the packaging, which offers great artwork featuring several scenes from the movie.

○ **£**20-30
○ **$**30-45

Arnold Schwarzenegger's action pictures have been hugely popular on video as well as at the cinema, but it is the *Terminator* movies that gave him what is perhaps his most celebrated role. Pictured here is a limited-edition boxed video of *Terminator 2* that is housed in a special tin casing; limited-edition releases usually offer unusual packaging as well as additional scenes from the movie. Not everyone agreed that the tin casing was a good idea – some fans who bought the video complained that it was rather fiddly to open. Nevertheless, a DVD of *Terminator 2* has since been released and it, too, came in a tin box.

Audio

Science-fiction and fantasy movies and TV programmes have given us not only action and excitement but also some memorable music. Even so, many of these themes have been regarded by music lovers with a degree of disdain, while for mainstream record collectors they are only of peripheral interest. However, there are record collectors who specialize in TV themes and film soundtracks. Musically, there is every reason to admire the work of many composers and musicians working in this field. To do it justice, the fantastic subject-matter of science-fiction and fantasy requires imaginative and inspirational music, and many composers have risen to the challenge. In doing so, they have often pushed back boundaries and explored the possibilities offered by new ways of making music – the work of the BBC Radiophonic Workshop, for example, is almost legendary. Even when the music is more kitsch than classic, it often typifies the period in which it was produced, which provides interest in itself. Because this music was not always taken seriously and is still not always appreciated, jumble sale finds are still possible. As with all collectibles, condition is important, and undamaged records with clean, intact sleeves will always be more desirable.

○ **£** 70-100
○ **$** 105-150

↑ *Thunderbirds Are Go* was the Tracy family's first big screen outing and was accompanied by this LP, which featured music from the Barry Gray Orchestra. The album includes the main theme plus incidental music. Gray was responsible for the music for many Gerry Anderson productions, going back to *Four Feather Falls* and *Supercar* in 1960. This LP is worth having for the cover-art alone, but it is a rare find.

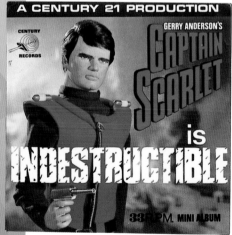

○ **£** 30-50
○ **$** 45-75

↑ Themes from Gerry Anderson productions were released as singles throughout the 1960s. In 1967 Century 21 Records released this EP, which includes the *Captain Scarlet* theme. A group called The Spectrum was created to record the theme song. Music trivia buffs may like to know that the drummer was Keith Forsey, who went on to find success as a producer and co-writer of the classic Simple Minds hit "Don't You Forget About Me".

The BBC Radiophonic Workshop was set up in the late 1950s, but it was the *Doctor Who* theme, created in 1963, that stands out as its best-known piece. Ron Grainer's theme was produced by Delia Derbyshire with the aid of a dozen oscillators to produce a distinctive sound that proved to be a landmark in the development of electronic music. This album was released in 1983 to coincide with a classic edition of the programme that featured all five actors to have played the role to date. It features music from the series plus, of course, that memorable theme.

○ £10-20
○ $15-30

The release of the *Star Wars* movie coincided with the height of the 1970s disco craze. This meant that it seemed like a good idea to produce disco versions of the music, as well as disco music inspired by the movie. The years have not been kind to the results, but perhaps that's just because disco quickly became very unfashionable and has yet to recover. Whatever the verdict of music history, the records themselves make interesting collectibles because they are unquestionably relics of their time.

○ £10-15
○ $15-22

○ £45-55
○ $68-82

The music for the movie *Tron* was provided by award-winning composer Wendy Carlos, whose 1968 LP *Switched on Bach*, which used Moog synthesizers, won huge critical and public acclaim. It went platinum and won three Grammy awards, helping to popularize electronic music in the process. Pictured here is a Japanese version of the soundtrack, which is the same as the version released elsewhere except for the red label on the record sleeve. This is a promotional album sent out to radio stations in Japan, and is a true rarity.

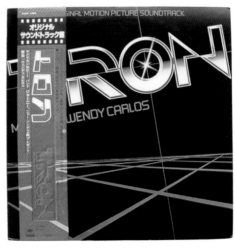

Miscellaneous

If videos, records, toys, and models seem rather predictable collectibles, there is a vast array of other products to choose from. Your favourite TV show or movie can be with you in almost every part of your life. To some, these products are pure kitsch, or even tacky, but to those who know and love them, they are a lot of fun. They can be serious and expensive fun too, as certain hard-to-find products can change hands for a lot of money. Lunchboxes, for example, are big business, and rumour has it that a vintage *Star Wars* lunchbox has great kudos among many a high-flyer in Silicon Valley. Part of the beauty of these miscellaneous licensed products is that they appeal to the collector who thought he or she had everything. So many products have been made that it is difficult, if not impossible, to keep up with them all. There are always surprises, and collectors may stumble across a toothbrush, hot-water bottle, or navel fluff remover that they never knew existed. Perhaps what's really interesting about these collectibles is the sheer imagination and ingenuity that can transform the most mundane objects into something that transcends their everyday function.

○ **£**25-30
○ **$**38-45

⬆ Interest in *Lost in Space* has cooled somewhat since the movie was released, and current prices reflect this. However, there have been persistent rumours of a new TV series with a completely new cast and, if they appear to be founded, then prices could recover sharply, especially if the new series becomes a big hit. The original 1960s version of the lunchbox shown here has changed hands for £300/$450, but this is a reproduction made in 1998 and is thus more affordable. It had a limited production run and sold out fast, so if you can find one it could prove a good investment.

○ **£**40-60
○ **$**60-90

⬆ *Star Wars* lunchboxes were made in many different designs for the original movies, and are still being made for the new ones. This *Return of the Jedi* lunchbox was produced in 1983 by Thermos, one of the most famous names in the market. It came with a flask inside, and the guide price assumes that this is present and the box is in excellent condition. Lunchboxes that show no signs of wear and tear are very hard to find, and without the flask might only be worth about £10–15/$15–22.

○ **£** 150-250
○ **$** 225-375

◀ The British firm of Recticel Sutcliffe helped to pioneer the use of rubberized materials in safe play areas for children in the late 1970s. They also made products such as this play mat that could help to protect carpets and furnishings from the popular modelling clay known as Play Doh, although it could of course also be used for general play as well. This play mat, measuring 60 x 96cm/24 x 38in, dates from 1983 and was made for the third *Star Wars* movie, *Return of the Jedi*. Featuring a scene that shows battles on the forest moon of Endor, the mat is rare today, and this is reflected in its price.

○ **£** 5-10
○ **$** 7.50-15

↑ Back in 1977, when playtime was over and you had finished cleaning up the galaxy, you could clean up in the tub with these *Star Wars* soaps. They were made in the UK by Cliro and modelled on the popular characters of R2D2 and C3PO. Packaging really makes a huge difference to the value of these items which, if they were not used, are likely to have been stored in bathrooms where damp and humidity will have taken its toll. In fact, it is arguably the case that the packaging would be of as much interest to collectors as the soaps themselves.

▼ *Harry Potter* is, in 2003, a worldwide phenomenon, but it should be remembered that the merchandising has been extensive, and collector interest is high. Some observers therefore feel that collectibles that are a little different will offer more collector interest and better investment value in the long term, not least because they could be overlooked. This Christmas decoration by Hallmark certainly offers something different – and it should be remembered that dedicated collectors of seasonal decorations may also find it desirable. This attractive ornament features the Mirror of Erised in which Harry sees his parents; the first Harry Potter movie was released in November 2001 and this was brought out for the Christmas of that year.

○ **£** 12-14
○ **$** 18-21

○ **£**150–200
○ **$**225–300

Dan Dare prompted a huge array of products during the 1950s, which was the heyday of this immensely popular British character. Dan Dare toys and other licensed products ranged from jigsaws and projectors to puppets, watches, and even wallpaper. The firm of Merit was responsible for many of these, such as this Space Control Radio Station. The boast on the box is that you can use it to send voice and code messages for up to half a mile, and it comes with a notepad and instructions. These can be missing, and this item is hard to find boxed and in good condition.

○ **£**250–300
○ **$**375–450

Dan Dare was a hit right from his introduction in 1950, and among the large amount of merchandise produced during the following decade was this pocket watch. A pocket watch might seem a little old-fashioned for a pilot of the future, but Ingersoll produced such an item in 1951. The second hand is in the form of a rocket and the watch bears the Eagle logo on the reverse. It would have been a prized possession for any boy lucky enough to have owned one, and would now be just as much appreciated by any modern-day collector.

○ **£**350–400
○ **$**525–600

The hi-tech gadgets that are associated with James Bond are a merchandising dream. The firm of A.C. Gilbert produced many Bond-related products during the 1960s, including watches, which have always lent themselves well to the 007 treatment. This intriguing James Bond Spy Watch is finished in silver with a blue, red, and white strap. Numerous Bond watches have been made since, but few can compare with this rarely seen item that would deserve pride of place in any Bond collection.

○ **£**90–100
○ **$**135–150

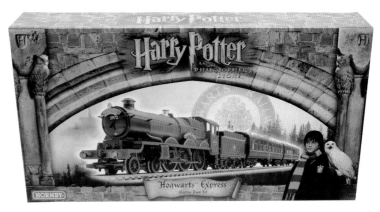

➥ Hornby is a very well-known company that has been producing train sets since the 1930s. The Hogwarts Express features prominently in the *Harry Potter* books and movies, and the firm was given the licence to produce a Hogwarts-style train set. Powered and operated by the standard Hornby train controller and transformer, the set includes a highly detailed Harry Potter "trakmat", plus "Hogsmead" station halt, platform, and assorted station accessories. This product will appeal to model-train buffs and Potter fans alike.

◀ James Bond may have been licensed to kill, but Corgi was licensed to produce toy die-cast versions of his Aston Martin DB5. However, that didn't stop other firms from getting in on the act, with unlicensed products such as this vehicle made by the Hong Kong firm Lincoln International. Ownership of the DB5 wasn't restricted to Bond, and legal problems are avoided because it does not claim to be Bond's car, although the "secret agent" tag leaves little room for doubt. Corgi DB5s came in different versions and can fetch as much as £400/$600 for an exceptional example. Unlicensed versions are also still collectible.

○ **£**200–250
○ **$**300–375

➥ The success of *The Lord of the Rings* movies has prompted a new wave of merchandise related to Tolkien's classic, but Middle Earth Toys were licensed to create products back in 1998, well before the movies were released. These figures of the characters were based directly on descriptions in the book and made to a detailed and accurate scale. They have been somewhat eclipsed by more recent licensed products, which range from pewter goblets to chess sets. The later products are certainly collectible, but these 1998 figures are getting hard to find, and are likely to become less affordable as time goes by.

○ **£**7–12
○ **$**10–18

Props & Promo

There is nothing like owning a piece of the action, and movie props allow you to do just that. Originally, props were not considered important outside movie-making, and were often discarded after shooting, although some were re-used in later productions. Those that survived did so because actors and crew members would help themselves to souvenirs. Today, props appear at auction almost as soon as a movie has finished shooting. Modest budgets are catered for, as even floor and wall tiles are sold. However, the most desirable props will always be those that capture the essence of a movie or TV show, and the more prominently they have featured on screen the better. Collectors also like the promotional items that were not made for release to the public, such as press books and press kits. They may lack glamour, but they are of great historical interest and the very fact that they were not made for the public adds kudos.

Props & Promo

Since props are now often readily available so soon after productions finish, there are always new opportunities for collectors. There are also lots of potential bargains; some films become milestones in cinema history while others are quickly forgotten, but it is not always instantly clear which category a film will fall into. Certain films start quietly, then gradually assume cult status – this has certainly been the case since the advent of video, which gives films a second chance to win an enthusiastic following. Authenticity is naturally very important in the props market, and the many reputable dealers in props and promotional material are aware of the need to authenticate their wares. The best way of doing this is through documentary evidence, such as letters from the studios, or even from the stars themselves. Such supporting evidence can also confirm that a given prop was the one actually used by a lead actor in the film, rather than by an extra – this naturally makes a huge difference to its value. Props are mostly bought for display purposes, and dealers often sell them suitably framed or cased. This has the added advantage of helping to protect the prop against damage.

◀ Steven Spielberg's *Close Encounters of the Third Kind* (1977) helped to spark a new wave of interest in the UFO phenomenon worldwide. This alien head is part of a costume that was used in the closing scenes in which the aliens finally make their long-awaited appearance. The costume consists of a sparkling stretch jumpsuit and a hand-painted rubber alien mask. It was sold at auction in 1999, accompanied by two letters of authenticity.

○ £1,800–3,000
○ $2,700–4,500

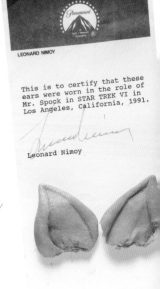

➡ The ears worn by Leonard Nimoy in the role of *Mr Spock* are arguably the most famous prosthetics in TV and movie history. This pair was used in *Star Trek VI: The Undiscovered Country* (1991), the last film to be made with the original-series cast. They were subsequently put up as a prize on the British TV show *The Big Breakfast* and the winner later sold them at auction. They benefit from an impressive provenance, being accompanied by a letter of authenticity signed by the actor who wore them.

○ £1,500–1,800
○ $2,250–2,700

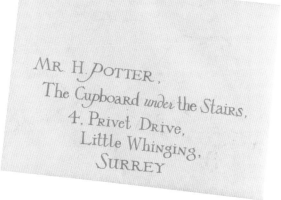

○ **£** 1,000–2,000
○ **$** 1,500–3,000

◄ *Waterworld* told the story of a future in which global warming has caused sea levels to rise and turned the world into a water planet where dry land is thought to be a myth. It was a very expensive movie featuring a star that had the Midas touch – and it was an embarrassing box-office flop. Nevertheless, props from flops can still be collectible. Although *Waterworld* seemed to damage Kevin Costner's career at the time, he remains very bankable, and this futuristic gun was used by Costner in the film. Made from moulded composite rubber, it is accompanied by a certificate of authenticity from the props company.

○ **£** 2,000–2,500
○ **$** 3,000–3,750

➡ Props are always interesting, but particularly so when they have played a key role in the movie. Nothing could be more important than the letter that informs the boy wizard that he has been accepted into Hogwarts School in *Harry Potter and the Philosopher's Stone* (2001). This prop letter, which is sealed, was sold at a recent auction together with supporting material. Included with the lot were copies of the contents of the envelope and a *USA Weekend* magazine cover of the movie's star, Daniel Radcliffe, as well as a letter from Warner Brothers confirming this as one of a small number of props donated to charity.

MR. H. POTTER,
The Cupboard under the Stairs,
4. Privet Drive,
Little Whinging,
SURREY

○ **£** 450–550
○ **$** 675–825

◄ Ray Harryhausen is one of the greatest names in fantasy movie-making, providing memorable special effects for classics such as *Jason and the Argonauts* (1963) and *Clash of the Titans* (1981). This shield came from the latter, which was Harryhausen's last movie. Made from fibreglass with hand-painted detail, it measures about 70cm/28in in diameter and is clearly visible in the movie, appearing in several key scenes. This is an extremely rare prop, and this particular example was recently offered by a dealer as the last one known to be in circulation.

○ **£**5,000–10,000
○ **$**7,500–15,000

The prop pictured here really needs no introduction: successfully combining malice with menace, the design for Darth Vader's helmet has rightfully become one of the iconic images of 20th-century cinema. This helmet is made of black fibreglass with see-through panels inserted into the cheek and neck areas. The perspex panels were intended to give better visibility to the wearer, who would have needed it because this prop is said to have been used in fighting scenes in all three of the original *Star Wars* films. This item therefore holds a place in cinema history that naturally doesn't come cheap.

○ **£**1,300–2,000
○ **$**1,950–3,000

One critic described *Blade Runner* as "looking like a fireworks display seen through fog". The murky gloom that was a trademark of the picture was illuminated in part by these umbrellas with glowing handles. They were seen throughout the movie, contributing to its visual style, and because they are so prominent, they are popular with collectors. A letter of authenticity from a member of the production team accompanied this example at auction. *Blade Runner* is such a cult classic that any genuine props associated with it are highly desirable.

The fantasy world of Xena, Warrior Princess required a large number of weapons of various shapes and sizes, many of which have since come onto the market. This sword, whose appearance alone would be enough to frighten any enemy, was used by the character Beserker in one of the episodes of this cult TV series. It is nearly 90cm/3ft long and has an impressive finish and outstanding attention to detail. A prop that has been used by Xena herself will always be more desirable and valuable but this "beserker" sword is still very collectible.

○ **£**400–450
○ **$**600–675

○ **£**1,500–2,000
○ **$**2,250–3,000

↑ "I'll be back", said Arnie – and so he was, in two sequels to date. This prop shotgun, made in composite material with metal strap loops, was used by Arnold Schwarzenegger in his role as the T-800 cyborg in the 1991 movie *Terminator 2*. It wasn't a subtle piece, but it certainly had plenty of action as the cyborg worked his way through a veritable armoury of weapons, including this one. Measuring 70cm/28in long, the gun is an impressive addition to any collection. This example comes with appropriate supporting paperwork.

○ **£**40–60
○ **$**60–90

◀ Press kits, as the name suggests, are intended for journalists and contain information that is designed to help them to write about the movie. A typical kit might contain a synopsis, photographs, and information on the cast and crew; consequently, they are popular with fans of the movie if they can get them. Different versions of press kits are often produced for different markets. The *Tron* kit shown here is an unusual version of the American press kit, containing some unique photographs.

○ **£**125–200
○ **$**190–300

➡ There are important differences between press books and press kits. The press kit was developed in the 1970s whereas the press book, designed for cinema owners rather than the media, is an older marketing tool. Its aim was to suggest ways of promoting the movie and it contained illustrations of various posters that could be ordered for the purpose. Press books are of limited appeal to collectors compared with, say, posters, but this information-packed British press book for *The War of the Worlds* (1953) is interesting because it is more elaborate than its American equivalent. Its cover also varies from the US poster artwork.

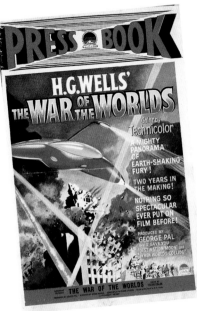

Ephemera

If something is described as "ephemeral", it means that it is only short-lived. In collecting circles ephemera refers to things that were not meant to be kept for any length of time, such as paper bags and packaging, and many ephemera collectibles are indeed made of paper. However, this definition is stretched by modern collecting habits – postcards are as likely to be collected as they are to be sent. Other items, from drinks cartons to cinema tickets, were clearly not made to be kept. Because most were thrown away, survivors can be collectible. While many collectors frown on indiscriminate hoarding, many people who really love *Lord of the Rings* or *Star Trek* want to keep practically anything to do with the subject. Autographs are usually bracketed with ephemera although they are rarely thrown away. Sometimes there is an obvious connection between autographs and ephemera – perhaps Harrison Ford has signed your *Star Wars* napkin!

Autographs

Autograph collecting is a well established hobby, but those long waits outside the stage door are not always necessary these days. This is particularly true if you are interested in sci-fi and fantasy stars and regularly attend fairs and conventions. Many actors attend these events, and queues at tables for autographs are common. Of course this has its down side. If a star regularly signs hundreds – or even thousands – of autographs, then they are likely to be of limited value, except of course to the fan who wants the autograph for its own sake. Autographs don't have to be signed in the traditional autograph book, or on trading cards as shown on these pages. Some stars are happy to sign anything for their fans, from underwear to inflatable sheep; Patricia Tallman, who plays a telepath in *Babylon 5*, recalled in a recent interview that she was once asked to autograph a fan's glass eye – she duly obliged! Autographs naturally vary in value according to whose they are, and the value of an autograph is likely to increase when we know that no more will be forthcoming. For example, the demise of DeForest Kelley and Gene Roddenberry can only make their autographs more collectible.

○ **£** 20-40
○ **$** 30-60

◀ Max Grodenchik has played various roles in TV shows, such as *Sliders*, while his movie credits include *Apollo 13* and *Rocketeer*. He was born in New York, but for the purpose of what is probably his best-known role to date, he hails from another planet. Here he is as Rom, the Ferengi in *Star Trek Deep Space Nine*, featured on a trading card from an autograph series that bears his signature. Some signed items by Max can be picked up for around £15/$22.50, but this card is also collectible in its own right and so the price reflects this.

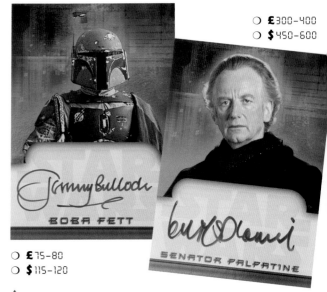

○ **£** 300-400
○ **$** 450-600

○ **£** 75-80
○ **$** 115-120

▲ Boba Fett the bounty hunter is one of the most enigmatic figures in the *Star Wars* movies and has a cult following among the fans. No wonder, then, that the signature of Jeremy Bullock, who plays the character, is considered such a prize. Ian McDiarmud plays Senator Palpatine and both these signatures are from a set of autographed *Star Wars* cards that were inserted into trading-card packs – the price of McDiarmud's card reflects the rarity of this particular example. Both signatures can be picked up elsewhere for as little as £20–50/$30–75.

○ **£**30-60
○ **$**45-90

George Clooney has a reputation for being one of the nice guys of Hollywood and is known to be very accommodating when fans ask for his autograph. What this does mean is that there are quite a few of his signatures about and they are not that difficult to obtain. On the other hand, it should be remembered that as Clooney is one of Hollywood's most bankable stars, his autograph is always sought after. This image shows Clooney and his co-star Chris O'Donnell in their respective roles as Batman and Robin in the 1997 movie; it is signed by both stars.

○ **£**20-40
○ **$**30-60

Former beauty queen Lynda Carter is an accomplished actress who has appeared in numerous movies and TV shows. However, her big break and most memorable role, and the one that propelled her to stardom, was that of Diana Prince/Wonder Woman in the 1970s TV series based on the 1940s comic strip. Lynda's autograph is by no means hard to find, but talk of a Wonder Woman revival could well enhance interest in this star's signature. In any case, for a true Wonder Woman fan, a signed photo of Lynda is a must.

Peter Jackson's epic production of *Lord of the Rings* boasted not only superb special effects, stunning scenery, and a great story, the latter courtesy of Professor Tolkien, but also a cast of international stars. There is a fair bit of autograph material available for all of them, understandably so when you consider the long and distinguished careers of certain cast members, such as Ian Holm and Ian McKellen. Autographs of rising stars such as Elijah Wood, who can surely look forward to a shining career, are always worth collecting. Shown here is a set of autographed cards issued for the first movie in the trilogy, *The Fellowship of the Ring*.

○ **£**40-100 (EACH)
○ **$**60-150 (EACH)

Other Ephemera

Some things are quite obviously collectible and desirable while others are not, and a lot of ephemera falls into the latter category. Yet it is precisely because people don't tend to think of preserving these things that they are discarded, and any surviving items go on to become desirable. A lot of ephemera appears in themed collections, which is to say that a *Star Wars* paper plate will find a place in the collection of a *Star Wars* fan – there probably are people who collect paper plates for their own sake, but they must be few and far between. Most items in this field are of little value, but of course that makes them all the more affordable. Because most ephemera is paper-based, you should look after it as you would other printed material; light and damp are the major concerns. Some people find ephemera a strange subject for a collection because it includes such everyday items as packaging. However, this is of great interest to students of design, and of course it makes valuable reference material. The biggest drawback is that it becomes easy to see the merit in just about everything and you could be tempted never to throw anything away.

❍ **£**150-200
❍ **$**225-300

🔺 Stamp collecting is a truly international hobby, but courtesy of Dan Dare it could be interplanetary as well. In the 1950s, users of Lever Brothers' Lifebuoy Soap could get this Dan Dare Interplanetary Stamp Folder free of charge with a postal offer. To fill it was a set of 32 mock postage stamps to collect; they were also given away with the soap, and purported to come from places such as Venus. The offer ran between 1953 and 1955 and, while they do come onto the market from time to time, it is very unusual to find examples such as this one, which is complete with all the stamps.

❍ **£**20-30
❍ **$**30-45

◀ Printed material of various kinds, including leaflets, flyers, and catalogues, are all desirable because they can provide valuable information on the products advertised. They are not just good to look at or interesting to browse through, they are also invaluable for anyone carrying out research. This is because they may include details of release dates for various models, as well as the original retail prices. Seen here is a 1960s Dinky Toys advertising leaflet that features models based on the *Thunderbirds* craft, alongside more conventional models from the range.

○ £8-12
○ $12-18

➡ For the true movie buff, attending an exclusive preview will always be a memorable experience, and the ticket is a tangible reminder of it. If you hold on to your ticket then it can have a collectible value as well, because it will be sought-after by fans of the movie as an interesting keepsake. Naturally, the more significant the movie, the more valuable the ticket will be. Shown here is a ticket for a special screening of the 1982 film *Tron*.

○ £110-130
○ $165-200

⬅ Science-fiction and fantasy movies and TV shows have spawned all kinds of toys and games for many decades. In the early 1980s, there was a new kind of game in town: the video arcade game. Because of its subject matter, *Tron* translated very well to this medium and Bally manufactured a game based on the movie. A video game tournament was organized to help promote both the game and the movie, and this is a poster that was issued to advertise the tournament. These posters are rare because they were produced for a limited event and were only issued for the weekend of the tournament.

○ £120-140
○ $180-210

➡ The current movie ratings of 18, 15, 12, and so on have become so familiar that it seems as if they have been with us forever. It is easy to forget that before 1982, the British cinema used a completely different set of ratings; you could only see an X certificate film if you were over 18. This is the original X-rated censor notice for the 1979 sci-fi/horror classic *Alien*. Measuring 30 x 35cm/12 x 14in, and suitably framed, this is not an everyday collectible, but what fan of this movie wouldn't want to own something like this?

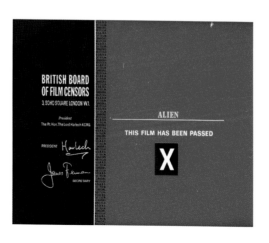

Bibliography, Sources, & Resources

Bibliography

Archer, Simon & Hearn, Marcus
What Made Thunderbirds Go:
The Authorised Biography
of Gerry Anderson
(BBC Consumer Publishing, 2002)

Cornwell, Sue & Kott, Mike
Star Trek Collectibles
(House of Collectibles, 1997)

Franks, Alan
Monsters and Vampires
(Octopus, 1976)

Walker, John (ed)
Halliwell's Film & Video Guide 2003
(HarperCollins Entertainment)

Wells, Stuart W.
Science Fiction Collectibles:
Identification and Price Guide
(Krause Publications, 1999)

Sources & Resources

Websites:
www.ebay.com
Online auctions

www.imdb.com
Internet Movie Database

www.janiancomics.com
Extensive comic site
Tel: 01908 609248

www.lambiek.net
Comics and info on artists

www.lostintoys.com
Lost in Space online museum & shop

www.megocentral.com
Information and history of Mego

www.posterprice.com
Prices & news about movie posters

www.robot1968.com
Toy robots for sale online

www.toyraygun.com
Fabulous site with a huge
selection of toy rayguns

www.toysrgus.com
Extensive Star Wars collectibles site

www.tron-sector.com
Valuable resource for all
things Tron

www.tvcentury21.com
Gerry Anderson site

Auctioneers:
Christie's New York
20 Rockefeller Plaza
New York
NY 10020
USA
Tel: 001 212 636 2000
www.christies.com

Christie's South Kensington
85 Old Brompton Road
London SW7 3LD
Tel: 020 7321 3281
www.christies.com

Cooper Owen
10 Denmark Street
London WC2H 8LS
Tel: 020 7240 4132
www.CooperOwen.com

Skinner Inc. Auctioneers
& Appraisers of Fine Art
357 Main Street
Bolton
MA 01740
USA
Tel: 001 978 779 6241
www.skinnerinc.com

Sotheby's
34-35 New Bond Street
London W1A 2AA
Tel: 020 7293 5000
www.sothebys.com

Vectis Auctions Limited
Fleck Way
Thornaby
Stockton-on-Tees TS17 9JZ
Tel: 01642 750616
www.vectis.co.uk

Dealers and Shops:
Assimilate This
Unit 65, The Peacocks
Causey Way, Woking
Surrey GU21 6GB
Tel: 01483 729923

Cards Inc.
Unit 9, Woodshots Meadow
Croxley Business Park
Watford WD18 8YU
Tel: 01923 200138
www.cardsinc.com

Forbidden Planet
71–75 New Oxford Street
London WC1A 1DG
Tel: 020 7836 4179
www.forbiddenplanet.com
There are 9 other branches across
England and a mail-order service

The Nostalgia Factory
51 North Margin Street
Boston
MA 02113
USA
Tel: 001 800 479 8754
www.nostalgia.com
Original movie posters & ephemera

Offworld
142 Market Halls
Arndale Center
Luton
Bedfordshire LU1 2TP
Tel: 01582 736256

The Prop Store of London
Great House Farm
Chenies, Rickmansworth
Hertfordshire WD3 6EP
Tel: 01494 766485
www.propstore.co.uk
The Prop Store of London is one
of the world's leading suppliers
of screen-used movie props and
costumes as collectible items. Their
warehouse and gallery are open
to visitors by appointment – phone
to organize a viewing, or browse
the extensive online catalogue.

Suffolk Sci-Fi and Fantasy
17 Norwich Road
Ipswich
Suffolk IP1 2ET
Tel: 01473 400655
www.suffolksci-fi.com

Wheels of Steel
(contact Jeff Williams)
Stand A12–13, Grays Antique Market
Unit B10 Basement
1–7 Davies Mews
London W1Y 2LP
Tel: 020 7629 2813

Zardoz Books
20 Whitecroft
Dilton Marsh
Westbury
Wiltshire BA13 4DJ
Tel: 01373 865371
www.zardozbooks.com

Publications:
Memorabilia
144 Southwark Street,
London SE1 0UP
Tel: 01536 764646
Monthly collectors' magazine

Model and Collectors Mart
1st Floor Edward House
Tindal Bridge
Edward Street
Birmingham B1 2RA
Tel: 0121 2338707
www.modelmart.co.uk
Monthly collectibles magazine

Starburst
Visual Imagination Limited
9 Blades Court
Deodar Road
London SW15 2NU
Tel: 020 8875 1520
and
Visual Imagination
PMB# 469
PO Box 6061
Sherman Oaks
CA 91413
USA
www.visimag.com/starburst
Monthly sci-fi and fantasy
entertainment magazine

Miscellaneous:
AFA Inc
Suite G 361
5805 State Bridge Rd
Duluth, GA 30097
USA
www.toygrader.com
Providers of impartial
action figure grading

Events:
Barry Potter Fairs
Tel: 01604 770025/01858 468459
www.barrypotterfairs.com
Regular toy and train collectors'
fairs around the UK

Collectormania
Middleton Hall
thecentre:mk
Midsummer Arcade
Central Milton Keynes
Buckinghamshire MK9 3BA
Tel: 01908 671138
www.showmastersonline.com/
collectormania.html
Regular collectors' fairs in the UK

London Expo
ExCel Centre
Royal Victoria Dock
London E16 1XL
Tel: 020 8523 1074
www.londonexpo.com
Sci-fi and collectors' fairs

Memorabilia
NEC Birmingham & SECC Glasgow
Tel: 0121 780 4141 (NEC)
    0141 248 3000 (SECC)
www.memorabilia.co.uk
Fair held several times
a year at both venues

Index

Acknowledgments

From the author:
Thanks are due to many people for their help in making this book a reality, including Martin Fisher for the Tron info, Ian Janian for his help with the comics section, and Maurice Flanagan for his advice on books, among a great many others. Thanks are also due to all at Miller's for their hard work, including Emily Anderson for guiding me through it all, and Anna Sanderson for giving me the chance to do it in the first place.

Photographic Acknowledgments Mitchell Beazley would like to thank the following for their contribution:
Front of jacket (clockwise from top left) Robert Opie; OPG/John & Simon Haley; OPG/S. Tanner/United Artists/EMI Archives; OPG; OPG/ S. Tanner/David Huxtable; **Back of jacket** Robert Opie; **1** OPG/David Huxtable, Alfie's Antique Market; **3** OPG/S. Tanner/Nostalgia Factory; **4** OPG/The Toy Store; **7** David Welch & John LaSpina; **8bl** Ronald Grant Archive; **8br** Vectis Auctions; **9bl** NASA; **9br** Skinner Inc.; **10** OPG/ Off World; **12tl** OPG/R. Saker/Suffolk Sci-Fi; **12br** OPG/Unicorn Antiques Centre; **13tr** OPG/Toy Boy, Alfie's Antique Market; **13cl** OPG/Toy Boy, Alfie's Antique Market; **13br** OPG/Dale Adams; **14** OPG/R. Saker/Off World; **15tl** OPG/Off World; **15tr** OPG/R. Saker/Off World; **15bl** OPG/Off World; **15br** OPG/Unicorn Antiques Centre; **16** OPG/Off World; **17tl** OPG/Off World; **17tr** OPG/R. Saker/Suffolk Sci-Fi; **17b** OPG/Private Collection; **18t** OPG/Private Collection; **18b** Assimilate This; **19tr** OPG/Toy Boy, Alfie's Antique Market; **19cl** Vectis Auctions; **19br** OPG/R. Saker/Suffolk Sci-Fi; **20** OPG/S. Tanner/Zardoz Books; **22–23** OPG/S. Tanner/Zardoz Books; **24tl** OPG/Ken Adlard; **24br** OPG/S. Tanner/Zardoz Books; **25** OPG/S. Tanner/Zardoz Books; **26–27** OPG/S. Tanner/Zardoz Books; **28–29** OPG/S. Tanner/Zardoz Books; **30** OPG/S. Tanner/Zardoz Books; **31tr & cl** OPG/S. Tanner/Zardoz Books; **31br** Martin Fisher; **32tl** OPG/Yorkshire Relics of Haworth; **32br** OPG/S. Tanner/Zardoz Books; **33tl** OPG/S. Tanner/Zardoz Books; **33cr** OPG/Roger Dixon/Phil Ellis; **33bl** OPG/S. Tanner/Zardoz Books; **34** OPG/R. Saker/Suffolk Sci-Fi; **36–37** Janian Comics; **38–39** Janian Comics; **40–41** Janian Comics; **42–43** Janian Comics; **44–45** Janian Comics; **46–47** Janian Comics; **48** OPG/ R. Saker/Off World; **50tl** Vectis Auctions; **50br** OPG/Collectors' Corner; **51tr** OPG/Thomas Wm Gaze & Sons; **51cl** Christie's Images; **51br** OPG/ Collectors' Corner; **52tl** OPG/David Huxtable, Alfie's Antique Market; **52cr** OPG/BBG Ambrose; **52bl** OPG/Off World; **53t** OPG/Thomas Wm Gaze & Sons; **53b** Martin Fisher; **54tl** OPG/Unicorn Antique Centre; **54cr** OPG/Childhood Memories; **54bl** OPG/Childhood Memories; **55tl** OPG/R. Saker/Off World; **55cr** OPG/Unicorn Antique Centre; **55bl & br** OPG/R. Saker/Off World; **56t** Christie's Images; **56b** Vectis Auctions; **57tl** OPG/R. Saker/Suffolk Sci-Fi; **57bl** OPG/Medway Auctions; **57br** Christie's Images; **58tl** OPG/The Toy Store; **58br** OPG/I. Booth/Christie's South Kensington; **59tl & cr** OPG/Off World; **59bl** OPG/R. Saker/Off World; **60tl** OPG/Rochester Antiques Centre; **60bl** OPG/Toy Boy, Alfie's Antique Market; **60br** OPG/R. Saker/Suffolk Sci-Fi; **61tl** Vectis Auctions; **61br** OPG/R. Saker/Off World; **62** Vectis Auctions; **63tl & cr** Vectis Auctions; **63bl** Martin Fisher; **64t** OPG/T. Ridley/Alfie's Antique Market; **64b** Skinner Inc.; **65tr** OPG/R. Saker/Off World; **65cl & bl** Vectis Auctions; **66tl** Martin Fisher; **66cr & bl** OPG/R. Saker/Suffolk Sci-Fi; **67tl** OPG/R. Saker/Suffolk Sci-Fi; **67cr** Vectis Auctions; **67bl** OPG/R. Saker/Suffolk Sci-Fi; **67br** OPG/R. Saker/Off World; **68t** OPG/John & Simon Haley; **68b** Vectis Auctions; **69** Vectis Auctions; **70tr** OPG/T. Ridley/Alfie's Antique Market; **70cl** OPG/Collectors' World; **70br** Vectis Auctions; **71tl** OPG/Off World; **71cr & bl** Vectis Auctions; **72–73** Vectis Auctions; **74t** OPG/ I. Booth/Alfie's Antique Market; **74b** Vectis Auctions; **75tr** OPG/R. Saker/Suffolk Sci-Fi; **75cl & br** Vectis Auctions; **76t** OPG/T. Ridley/Alfie's Antique Market; **76b** Vectis Auctions; **77tl** OPG/R. Saker/Off World; **77cr** OPG/R. Saker/Suffolk Sci-Fi; **77b** Christie's Images; **78** OPG/S. Tanner/Cards Inc.; **80–81** OPG/S. Tanner/Cards Inc.; **82** OPG/R. Saker/Suffolk Sci-Fi; **83tl & cr** OPG/S. Tanner/Cards Inc.; **83bl** OPG/R. Saker/Suffolk Sci-Fi; **84** OPG/ R. Saker/Suffolk Sci-Fi; **85tl** OPG/R. Saker/Suffolk Sci-Fi; **85tr** OPG/S. Tanner/Cards Inc.; **85br** OPG/R. Saker/Suffolk Sci-Fi; **86t** OPG/R. Saker/ Suffolk Sci-Fi; **86b** OPG/S. Tanner/Cards Inc.; **87tl** OPG/R. Saker/Suffolk Sci-Fi; **87cr** OPG/S. Tanner/Cards Inc.; **87bl** Martin Fisher; **88** OPG/ R. Saker/Suffolk Sci-Fi; **89tr** OPG/Private Collection; **89cl & br** OPG/R. Saker/Suffolk Sci-Fi; **90** OPG/S. Tanner/Nostalgia Factory; **92** OPG/S. Tanner/ Nostalgia Factory; **93tl** Christie's Images; **93tr** Skinner Inc., Auctioneers & Appraisers of Antiques & Fine Art, Bolton MA; **93bl & br** Christie's Images; **94tl** Skinner Inc.; **94cr & bl** Christie's Images; **95tr** Christie's Images; **95cl** Skinner Inc.; **95bl** OPG/S. Tanner/Nostalgia Factory; **95br** Christie's Images; **96tl** Christie's Images; **96tr** Skinner Inc.; **96bl** Christie's Images; **96br** Skinner Inc.; **97tr** OPG/S. Tanner/Nostalgia Factory; **97cl & br** Skinner Inc.; **98tl** Christie's Images; **98bl** OPG/The Reel Poster Gallery; **98br** OPG/S. Tanner/Nostalgia Factory; **99** OPG/S. Tanner/ Nostalgia Factory; **100** Vectis Auctions; **102t** Assimilate This; **102b** Martin Fisher; **103tl** Martin Fisher; **103c & bl** Vectis Auctions; **104t** OPG/S. Tanner/United Artists/EMI Archives; **104b** OPG/T. Ridley/Memory Lane; **105tr** OPG/S. Tanner/BBC/EMI Archives; **105cl** OPG/S. Tanner/Splash/ John Stanley; **105br** Martin Fisher; **106t** OPG/R. Saker/ Suffolk Sci-Fi; **106b** Vectis Auctions; **107tl** OPG/R. Saker/Suffolk Sci-Fi; **107cl** OPG/S. Tanner/David Huxtable; **107br** Assimilate This; **108** Vectis Auctions; **109tr** OPG/Wheels of Steel; **109cl** Vectis Auctions; **109br** Assimilate This; **110** The Prop Store of London; **112t** Christie's Images; **112b** Sotheby's; **113tl & cr** Sotheby's; **113bl** The Prop Store of London; **114tl & cl** Christie's Images; **114b** The Prop Store of London; **115tl** Sotheby's; **115cl** Martin Fisher; **115br** Christie's Images; **116** OPG/R. Saker/Suffolk Sci-Fi; **118** OPG/R. Saker/Suffolk Sci-Fi; **119tl** OPG/Cooper Owen; **119cr** Vectis Auctions; **119b** OPG/R. Saker/Suffolk Sci-Fi; **120** Vectis Auctions; **121tr & cl** Martin Fisher; **121br** OPG/Cooper Owen.